Ministering
Inner Healing
Biblically
(That You and Others May Be Healed)

by Betty Tapscott

Tapscott Ministries
P.O. Box 19827
Houston, TX 77224 U.S.A.

Many thanks and much appreciation to my secretary, Elizabeth Rincon, who faithfully typed and retyped the manuscript. Thanks to Joe Van Cloostere (office manager at Tapscott Ministries), Shirley Stansbery, Laurie Ford, and Lois Livesay for all their help in proofreading, and for their encouragement, support, and love.

Scripture quotations are used with permission from:

The Living Bible, paraphrased, copyright © 1975 by Tyndale House Publishers, Wheaton, Illinois.

The New Catholic Study Bible, St. Jerome Edition © 1985 by Thomas Nelson, Inc.

The New International Version of the Bible, published by the Zondervan Corporation, copyright © 1978 by the New York International Bible Society.

The Jerusalem Bible, © 1966, 1967, and 1968 by Darton, Longman and Todd Ltd. and Doubleday and Company, Inc.

The Revised Standard Version of the Bible (RSV), copyright © 1973 by the Division of Christian Education of the National Council of Churches of Christ in the U.S.A.

The Amplified Bible, © 1965 by Zondervan Publishing House.

Revised edition December 1987.

DEDICATED WITH LOVE . . .

To my children and their chosen ones, my parents, and my extended family. I'm thankful and I praise God for all of you. I am grateful and blessed that you each know Jesus as your Personal Savior. You are each so special to me and I love you.

FOREWORD

Inner healing is a bridge between "here" and "there." Where is "here" and "there"? It's where you are right now, and where you need to be. Inner healing is the bridge you can walk over to get "there."

This book is double purposed because it teaches you how to minister inner healing and how to be healed yourself.

Charles and Frances Hunter
Houston, Texas

Ministering Inner Healing Biblically is a much needed book for those involved in prayer counseling or for those who need inner healing themselves.

It includes biblical guidelines that will help each person reach the goals of inner healing — WHOLENESS: Spirit, Soul, and Body.

As you read this book, may the healing Jesus permeate you, set you free, and transform you.

Fr. Robert DeGrandis
New Orleans, Louisiana

Betty Tapscott is a special person . . . the love and presence of Jesus shine through her.

Each person with a ministry of Inner Healing Prayer is like a different colored thread running through a beautiful tapestry that can only be completed when all of them are woven together. This lovely "fabric" is enhanced by the gifts Betty brings to it.

Over the years I've recommended her first book, *Inner Healing Through Healing of Memories,* and I will now, also, be recommending this one.

Rita Bennett
Edmonds, Washington

I'm impressed with Betty Tapscott's new book for the following five reasons:

(1) It's practical. This is a day when the Christian church is being deluged with "how-to" books. This edition by Betty Tapscott deals with real-life situations. All the practical suggestions are a result of experience by a lady who has been there. She knows what is workable and what is non-workable. Her ideas are a result of a fruitful and productive ministry.

(2) It's Biblical. She avoids New Age teachings, metaphysical approaches and holistic psychological logic. The Bible is her book. She lives in it and it lives in her.

(3) Her book is readable. I was delighted at the format and how easy it was to read.

(4) Her book is quotable. I'm using illustrations from her book. Her background gives validity to her illustrations.

(5) This book is durable. It is going to be around for a long, long time.

Dick Mills
Hemet, California

INTRODUCTION

This book is certainly not intended to be a textbook on prayer counseling. There will be many areas not even touched upon, and other areas covered only slightly.

The main purpose in writing this book comes from numerous requests to do so. Often after I've finished a seminar on inner healing and given a talk to counselors or "soon-to-be" counselors, many have said, "Do you have those guidelines in a book form?" The answer was always, "No!"

"Please put them in writing for us," they would say.

So — here they are!

Again, let me reiterate: This book is only the "briefest of brief," and a very simplistic form of some do's and don'ts. However, I've found these guidelines invaluable in over fifteen years of ministering inner healing.

I might add that I have an M.Ed. in psychology, but that does not really prepare one for prayer counseling and praying for inner healing through healing of memories. Only the Holy Spirit can do the in-depth work that has to be done in order that the wounded can be healed.

As you are reading this book, you may be involved in inner healing. Or, you may have a keen interest in it, and feel that the Lord is leading you into this area of ministry. Or, you may be hurting deeply yourself, and crying out to the Lord, "Oh, God, please heal me. Please heal my own broken heart and wounded spirit even as I pray for others." Whatever the case may be, my friend, may God bless you and the people that you pray with. May you each receive that healing touch from Jesus that He provides through the ministry of inner healing. Happy and blessed counseling.

In His Love,

Betty Tapscott
P.O. Box 19827
Houston, Texas 77224 U.S.A.
May 1987

TAPSCOTT BOOKS

Inner Healing Through Healing of Memories
(German: *Innere Heilung*)
(Portuguese: *Cura Interior*)

Set Free
(German: *Frei Gemacht . . . !*)

Fruit of the Spirit

Out of the Valley
(German: *Licht im dunklen Tal*)

*Forgiveness and Inner Healing**
(Spanish: *Perdonar Y Sanidad Interior**)

*Healing of Self-Image**

*Coauthored with Fr. Robert DeGrandis

CONTENTS

Introduction

Foreword

1. Inner Healing and the Bible 1
   (That You and Others May Be Healed)

2. The Two Steps of Inner Healing 13

3. Your Spiritual Covering 37

4. Cardinal Rules 45

5. Prayer Counselors 52

6. The Compassionate Prayer 69

7. B.L.T. — Please 75

8. Ministering Do's 81

9. Ministering Don'ts 93

10. The Counseling Session 109

11. How to Keep Your Inner Healing 121

12. Words of Caution 129

13. How to Prevent Burnout 133

14. A Call From God 140

15. The Story of Eva 165

Appendix I:
   Psychology/Church Counseling? 173

Appendix II:
   Basic Guidelines for Inner Healing 175

Appendix III:
   Scriptures on Inner Healing 176

Appendix IV:
   Recommended Reading 182

CHAPTER ONE

INNER HEALING AND THE BIBLE
(THAT YOU AND OTHERS MAY BE HEALED)

*"The Spirit of the Lord is upon me; he has ap-
pointed me to preach Good News to the poor, he
has sent me to heal the brokenhearted and to
announce that captives shall be released and the
blind shall see, that the downtrodden shall be
freed from their oppressors, and that God is
ready to give blessings to all who come to him"*
(Luke 4:18-19, TLB).

For those who may question the validity
or need of inner healing, please just walk
in the shoes of this mother for a moment, my friend.

A letter came to the Tapscott Ministries office one day from a mother in a southern state. Her tragic story broke our hearts.[1]

Her young teenage son had been emotionally ill over a period of years, and she had faithfully and staunchly stood in prayer for him for complete healing, loving him all the time, and doing everything possible to help him.

One day he took a shotgun and put it to his head in his mother's and father's bedroom, and ended his life. She was in their bathroom, with no idea of what was about to take place, when she heard the deafening blast of the shotgun. She ran a few steps and opened the door. There was bloody body tissue on the floor, ceiling, and on her clothes in the open closet.

She frantically knelt by her son, and with unbelief and terror in her heart, she looked at the mortal wound. Then she looked deeply into his eyes, and for a brief second she saw the wholesome look of the son she knew before his mental illness. She saw a look of Jesus in his eyes — and then he was gone.

This mother felt like Job did. *"My heart is broken. Depression haunts my days. My weary nights*

[1]Since her first letter, my staff and I have talked to her by phone many times and have had the privilege of meeting and praying with her at the Hunter Healing Explosions. She is a precious saint in the Lord.

are filled with pain as though something were relent-
lessly gnawing at my bones. All night long I toss and
turn and my garments bind about me" (Job 30:16-18,
TLB).

WHAT WERE SOME OF THE STATEMENTS
MADE TO THIS MOTHER?

— "Just have faith, friend! Everything will be
all right."

— "Just praise God! You'll be over it soon."

— "Don't cry, dear. Christians don't cry." Or,
the most painful statement of all,

— "But, really, isn't he much better off now?"

People in grief do not need responses like some
of these that were given without thought or sensitivity. These supposedly "helpful" comments did
not help — they hurt, very deeply.

WHAT WERE SOME OF THE
QUESTIONS THAT THIS BROKENHEARTED
MOTHER RECEIVED?

— "You really should be over your grief by
now; why, it's been six months since the
death of your loved one, hasn't it?"

— "With your faith, how do you explain what happened?"

— "Doesn't this make you mad at God?"

— "Do you think you did everything possible to help your son?" Or,

— This question may not have been asked, perhaps only implied — "What sin in your family do you suppose caused this tragedy?"

These stabbing questions (and others) heaped guilt and were like searing arrows piercing her already wounded spirit. The Word says, *"What you say can preserve life or destroy it . . ."* (Proverbs 18:21, JSB). She was almost destroyed by people's comments.

This godly, Spirit-filled, grieving mother is praying in the Spirit, praising, forgiving, staying in the Word, and attending church regularly; but her heart is broken, her mind overwhelmed with the tragedy she encountered. The ghastly memory of her son lying in a pool of blood, his head shattered, is almost more than she can physically or emotionally handle.

WHAT DOES THIS GRIEVING MOTHER NEED?

She needs the loving arms of family and friends. She needs a shoulder to cry on, gentle hugs, and warm handshakes. She needs the healing power of Jesus most of all, but, she also needs someone to listen to her compassionately as she pours out her deepest hurts from her shattered and broken heart. God uses time and friends to help bring about His healing of broken hearts.

SHE NEEDS INNER HEALING!

She needs prayer for the healing of a memory that is so horrible that only the healing power of Jesus could ever erase the pain.

> **Inner healing does not take away the memory completely, but takes away the pain. Inner healing (healing of memories) is not a one-time experience, but a continuing process.**

Her heart's cry is like David's, *"I weep with grief; my heart is heavy with sorrow; encourage and cheer me with your words"* (Psalm 119:28, TLB).

"Your words" — the words of the Lord!

"Our words" — words we hear from the Holy Spirit and bring forth to share in the prayer for healing of memories with those whose hearts are hurting. Hurting not only because of a death but perhaps from broken marriages, relationships, dreams, shattered reputations. And other deep losses such as a loss of business, loss of life's savings, jobs, or promotions.

"Words" — that will bring the life of Jesus, the love of Jesus, and the light of Jesus. *"You have turned on my light! The Lord my God has made my darkness turn to light"* (Psalm 18:28, TLB). *". . . I am the Lord who heals you"* (Exodus 15:26, TLB).

WHAT IS INNER HEALING, AND IS IT BIBLICAL?

Inner healing is the healing of the inner man: the mind, the emotions, the painful memories, the wounded spirit. It is the process of being set free from all bondage. *Yes, it is biblical!* We are three parts: spirit, soul, and body; and God wants to heal the whole person: spiritually, emotionally, and physically.

> *"May the God of peace himself make you entirely pure and devoted to God; and may your **spirit** and **soul** and **body** be kept strong and blameless until that day when our Lord Jesus Christ comes back again"* (1 Thessalonians 5:23, TLB).

> *". . . he was wounded and bruised for our sins. He was chastised that we might have peace; he was lashed and we were healed!"* (Isaiah 53:5, TLB).

Inner healing is basically: FORGIVENESS and RECONCILIATION, and, as a reminder to all who are involved in this ministry of our Lord, our Cornerstone of beliefs should always be:

6

1. Inner healing is the promise that, *"He heals the brokenhearted, binding up their wounds"* (Psalm 147:3, TLB).

2. Inner healing is the experience of a counselor listening as a person pours out the hurts of a broken heart, a confused mind, or a shattered personality.

3. It is the experience when a counselor prays with a person over each bondage, asking the Lord to set him free of anger, depression, rejection, unforgiveness, fear, suicide, etc.

4. It is the experience of the counselor praying and asking the Lord to heal all of the person's painful memories.

5. Inner healing is knowing and believing that Jesus Christ introduced into any situation brings healing. *"Jesus Christ is the same yesterday, today and forever"* (Hebrews 13:8, TLB).

6. Inner healing must be completely of the Lord. It should never even hint of mysticism, hypnotism, anything psychic, mind control, mind sciences, any Eastern religion, or cults.

7. Inner healing should never be so steeped in symbolism or visualization that we lose the basic simplicity of Jesus Christ.

8. Inner healing should never be grounded in liberal or humanistic psychiatry, or where the prevailing attitude is, "Do your own thing if it

makes you happy and feels good." This un-christian attitude is flirting with danger and could lead to spiritual and emotional chaos and destruction. However . . .

> **As a Prayer Counselor, we should never shun good, sound, Christian psychology and basic mental health principles.**
>
> **Praise God for those Christian psychologists, psychiatrists, and counselors who use their expertise in finding out what the problem is and then recognizing that it is God's healing power that sets people free and heals them.**
>
> **How sad to hear enormously anointed men of God on television saying, "There is *no* Christian psychology; the two cannot go together." How degrading to the thousands of godly men and women who bring hurting people to the throne of Jesus Christ through Bible-based counseling.**

9. In inner healing we must always keep our eyes on Jesus and not on Satan. We must not become too top-heavy in deliverance, for example, and look for a demon behind every door or a spirit behind every sneeze.

10. In inner healing we must always remember that Christians cannot be possessed — only oppressed.

11. Inner healing never did and never will take the place of true REPENTANCE in our lives.

12. Inner healing has as its firm foundation — FORGIVENESS. That is the *key* of all emotional healing. Forgiveness — of **others, ourselves,** and **God.** (God is sovereign and does no wrong, but people often blame Him for their failures and tragedies. They may have anger and resentment toward God, which is a symptom of unforgiveness.) They must forgive and repent.

13. Inner healing is not a one-time experience, but a process.

14. Inner healing is not digging and delving in the garbage of the past, but asking Jesus to throw away the garbage and even to remove the "stench of the past." The Bible says, *"Forget the past and look forward to what lies ahead"* (see Philippians 3:13, TLB), but we cannot do that if we keep living in the past and hanging on to and carrying with us rotting emotional debris.

———

I like what Dr. David Seamands wrote in his book, *Healing of Memories.* Chapter 5 is entitled "Biblical Foundations for Memory Healing."[2]

[2]Dr. David Seamands, *Healing of Memories,* Victor Books (Wheaton, IL, 1985), pp. 61-62. Used with publisher's permission.

9

"It is of utmost importance to understand that the healing of memories has a solid foundation in the Scripture, which is our final authority in all matters of faith and practice. Some people have totally rejected all forms of inner healing because the precise definitions do not appear in the Bible. If we applied that reasoning to everything, we could be led to fanatical and even dangerous extremes — not wearing clothes with buttons; not driving cars; not using pianos, organs, or PA systems in church; refusing penicillin for a sick child and thus being the cause of his death. We would actually be denying that all truth comes from God and that we have a spiritual obligation to use every new insight and discovery in any area of life for God's glory and human good. The real question is not whether a practice appears in the Bible in the specific form or language we use today. Rather, the question is whether it is contradictory to or consistent with principles stated in Scripture. In accordance with this basic tenet, we Christians are grateful for all the new truths, insights, and discoveries which continually come to us from many fields such as medicine, sociology, mathematics, physics, and psychology. As we look at the biblical teachings, we find the principles upon which we base the healing of memories."

EMOTIONAL WOUNDS CAN LEAD
TO PHYSICAL PROBLEMS

There have been people who were bleeding internally and they were not aware of their problem. Life's blood was draining from them. They were weak and anemic. They could have bled to death without the surgeon's skill to stop the bleeding.

There are also people "bleeding to death" emotionally. They are wounded and bruised, shattered and scarred. Life is practically draining from them because their spirit has been so wounded. They desperately need a spiritual blood transfusion. They need life; they need help. Tragically, many times those around them don't even notice that they are emotionally wounded, bleeding, and dying.

Surgeons can stop internal physical bleeding, but only Jesus can heal a broken and bleeding heart. He wants to use us, however, as His instrument to minister the needed emotional healing — inner healing. He wants us to help pick up the shattered pieces and to help mend a crushed and broken heart.

In the *Journal of the American Medical Association* (and quoted in Orange, California, A.P.), Dr. Michael Brodsky wrote: "Stress from emotional trauma can lead the heart to failure. . . . An emotionally broken heart can really kill you. The effects of stress might explain why a person whose spouse

11

dies has a high risk of death in the year after the funeral. In many cases emotional support is very important in preventing a physically broken heart."[3]

Dr. Messenger wrote in his book:

"When we experience physical pain that is more than our nervous system can handle, we will faint or pass out. Likewise, when we experience an emotional hurt greater than our ability to cope, our mind will short-circuit the pain and suppress it into our subconscious.

"But the suppression is not a long-term answer. Though it may be the only way to cope with the immediate shock to our emotions, it doesn't really deal with the problem; it merely postpones it. Suppressing emotional hurts deep inside is like putting the lid on a pressure cooker and turning up the burner. The pressure builds and will be expressed through our body one way or another. It may come out either in verbally expressed emotions or be diverted into disease in the stomach, colon, heart, lungs, or elsewhere."[4]

Inner healing, or healing of memories, is part of the gift to us for which Jesus paid the price. It is our GIFT. We only have to receive it. *"I am leaving you with a gift — peace of mind and heart . . ."* (John 14:27, TLB).

[3]*Journal of the American Medical Association,* article by Dr. Michael Brodsky. Quoted in Orange, California, A.P.

[4]*Dr. Messenger's Guide to Better Health,* © 1981. Dr. David L. Messenger, Old Tappan, New Jersey; Fleming Revell Co.

CHAPTER TWO

THE TWO STEPS OF INNER HEALING

"Oh, Lord, you have freed me from my bonds and I will serve you forever. I will worship you and offer you a sacrifice of thanksgiving" (Psalm 116:16-17, TLB).

God leads each person into ministry in a different way. In chapter 1 of my book, *Inner Healing Through Healing of Memories,*[1] I share exactly how the Lord literally pushed me into the ministry of inner healing. He actually gave me the two steps of inner healing that He wanted me to use and these steps are listed, along with the inner healing prayers and Scriptures, in that book.

If the ministry of inner healing (forgiveness and reconciliation) is based on Jesus Christ and His Word, then there is no absolutely "wrong" way or

[1]*Inner Healing Through Healing of Memories* © 1975 by Betty Tapscott, may be ordered from Tapscott Ministries, P.O. Box 19827, Houston, TX 77224.

"right" way of ministering. If you're ministering in the anointing and power of the Holy Spirit, He may direct you to minister a different way each time you pray for inner healing. The Word says that **it is His anointing that breaks the yoke.** (See Isaiah 10:27, KJV.) We must always remember this, and give Him all praise and glory.

Certainly there are no hard and fast rules on how you are to minister. Your teacher must be the Holy Spirit. I agree 100% with Dr. Seamands,[2] who wrote, "The healing of memories is not a cure-all for every emotional and spiritual hang-up" and "memory healing is only a form of spiritual therapy."

We cannot box God in, we cannot limit Him! We cannot program the Holy Spirit like a computer.

Remember —

The following two steps are only SUGGESTIONS for ministering inner healing.

STEP 1
PRAYER FOR BINDING AND CASTING OUT UNCLEAN SPIRITS

(HOW TO DO SPIRITUAL WARFARE)

". . . whatever you bind on earth is bound in heaven, and whatever you free on earth is freed in heaven" (Matthew 18:18, TLB).

[2]Seamands, op. cit., p. 188.

The Two Steps of Inner Healing

The Lord taught me in the ministry of inner healing to first bind and cast out each unclean spirit. The names are given by the Lord through Word of Knowledge and through the Gift of Discernment.

And to the age-old question, "Is it a spirit or is it not?" If the emotional wound is not healed, why isn't it healed? Wouldn't it be because it is infected and there is still some foreign matter in the wound? This principle comes from the natural application. If a physical wound is not cleansed of all dirt and germs, the wound will become infected and will not heal properly. It will become very painful. In both situations (physical and emotional) the wounds must be cleansed. Perhaps the infection is caused by: bitterness, hate, anger, resentment, guilt, rejection, depression, unforgiveness, etc.?

I have heard Charles and Frances Hunter say so many times, "When in doubt — cast it out!"

Steve, my eldest son, who is in full-time ministry working with heroin addicts at The Carpenter's Workshop, the center he founded and directs, made a very interesting and thought-provoking statement. "Man can mess up the best laid plans of God or Satan." How true! "When a person has an emotional hurt, it does not presuppose that it is demonic; it does presuppose, however, that we have not allowed God to work in our lives to heal the hurt."

There are several Scriptures about binding and casting out the unclean spirits.

". . . whatever you bind on earth is bound in heaven, and whatever you free on earth will be freed in heaven" (Matthew 18:18, TLB).

"One cannot rob Satan's kingdom without first binding Satan. Only then can his demons be cast out!" (Matthew 12:29, TLB).

"For God will break the chains that bind his people and the whip that scourges them . . ." (Isaiah 9:4, TLB).

The Bible also says,

". . . Resist the devil and he will flee from you . . ." (James 4:7b, TLB).

"He sent his word and healed them and delivered them from their destructions" (Psalm 107:20, KJV).

I usually have the person repeat the commands after me. I want them to realize that they can do this by themselves. I want them to know that:

". . . greater is he that is in you, than he that is in the world" (1 John 4:4, KJV), and

". . . where the Spirit of the Lord is, there is liberty" (2 Corinthians 3:17, KJV).

With the knowledge of these Scriptures, the counselee will be able to take authority over the evil one when he or she has an anxiety attack and say, "Spirit of fear, you are bound and cast out in the name of Jesus. Lord Jesus, please release Your love and peace in me."

I want them to be able to quote the Scripture, *"For God has not given us a spirit of fear, but of power, and of love and of a sound mind"* (2 Timothy 1:7, NKJV). I want the counselees to discover that they can be set free because of the power and authority of Jesus in them.

As I continue ministering, I keep having the person call out each spirit as the Holy Spirit reveals them to me. I want them to continually verbalize with me. For example:

"Spirit of rejection, you are bound and cast out in the name of Jesus."

"Spirit of depression, you are bound and cast out in the name of Jesus."

"Spirit of bitterness, you are bound and cast out in the name of Jesus."

As the counselor, we must take time to listen to the Holy Spirit reveal every unclean spirit and have the person ask God to set them free from every bondage — name or unnamed, large or small.

We must, in the name of Jesus, cut with the sword of the Spirit, every spell, verbal curse, hex, inner vow, and any bondage of the occult.

After each unclean spirit is cast out, it is helpful to also ask the Lord to release His corresponding healing spirit.

For example: In the name of Jesus, I

— Bind the spirit of unforgiveness — Lord Jesus, release Your spirit of forgiveness.

— Bind the spirit of grief — Lord, release Your spirit of joy and gladness.

— Bind the spirit of nervousness — Lord, release Your serenity and calmness.

— Bind the spirit of unclean thoughts — Lord, release pure, wholesome thoughts.

— Bind the spirit of prejudice — Lord, release the spirit of tolerance.

— Bind the spirit of anger — Lord, release Your spirit of peace.

Finally, after the counselee's temple is cleansed, be certain to ask the Lord to fill it to overflowing with the Holy Spirit and all the fruit of the Spirit: *". . . love, joy, peace, patience, kindness, goodness, faithfulness, gentleness and self-control"* (Galatians 5:22, TLB).

After the binding and casting out process, then you are ready for Step 2 of inner healing. Please remember that these are very short and simplified explanations of the steps in inner healing.

18

STEP 2
PRAYER FOR HEALING OF MEMORIES

"I knew you before you were formed within your mother's womb . . ." (Jeremiah 1:5, TLB).

In praying for the healing of memories, I was led by the Lord to pray very *simply.* I pray that the oil of the Holy Spirit cleanse the painful emotional wounds, and then I pray asking Jesus to heal the hurts, the woundedness, and brokenness. I was not led to use a lot of visualization or symbolism.

It depends on the time available as to how detailed you can be in praying for healing of memories. Also, it depends on how wounded the person is. It may take more than one session to complete the prayer for healing of memories.

Remember — *This is only a sample prayer.* Many situations are not included at all; others only briefly. This is why it is absolutely imperative that a counselor rely on the Holy Spirit to reveal each person's deep emotional hurts.

Usually, the Lord leads me to pray in the following manner:

19

ANCESTRAL HEALING[3]

"Lord Jesus, go all the way back into the third and fourth generation, and even to the beginning of time. The Word says, *'. . . for I the Lord thy God am a jealous God, visiting the iniquity of the fathers upon the children unto the third and fourth generation . . .'* (Exodus 20:5, KJV). Lord, break all spells, curses, hexes; and any inner vows not of You. Lord, set this person free from generations of bondage in the occult (see Leviticus 19:31; 20:6, TLB). Heal the family blood lines, Lord Jesus, and we ask that You would do generational (ancestral) healing.

"Lord Jesus, break all harmful genetic ties (for inherited diseases), and all harmful emotional ties (mental illness, psychosis, fears, anger, unforgiveness, depression, and suicide).

"Dear Lord, cleanse the family blood lines. This is especially necessary when there was addiction to alcoholism, or in the case of inherited physical diseases.

"Dear Lord, cleanse the family blood line of any curse of incest, child abuse, pornography, prostitution, homosexuality, lesbianism, nymphomania, or any other form of sexual perversion."

---

[3]Please understand that this is a very abbreviated and simplistic form of the prayer for generational healing or ancestral healing. In no way do these two paragraphs go into the depth of those prayers. In no way is this associated with praying for the dead. Ancestral healing should never be done in any way to raise the slightest question or hint of reincarnation.

IN THE WOMB

"Dear Lord, You were there from before the world began. You knew about each person being formed in his mother's womb." (See Psalm 139:13-16, TLB).

"If the mother had a previous abortion, miscarriage, or a stillborn baby, it is important to pray that she be set free from the spirit of grief. In the case of abortion, we need to pray for the spirit of murder and the cleansing of the womb."

In whatever way the mother lost her baby, we should pray for any harmful, emotional soul ties to be broken between her and the baby. We need to pray that she releases that baby completely to the Lord. She needs to forgive and accept forgiveness.

"Lord, if they were conceived in rape (even rape in marriage), anger, alcoholic stupor, in any other state except a beautiful, loving, and wholesome experience within marriage — dear Lord, please cleanse and heal.

"While the baby was in the womb those first three months, if the mother considered abortion, Lord, heal any rejection or fear in the baby.

"Jesus, heal any trauma that occurred in the uterus during the first six months: from surgery because of cancer, threatened miscarriage, car accident, being beaten by the husband, or some other trauma to the womb and baby.

"Lord Jesus, during the seventh, eighth, and ninth months until birth, we ask that You would heal any negative emotion that the unborn baby felt from the mother. Heal the memories of the discomfort the baby felt when the mother smoked."[4]

AT BIRTH

"If the mother started labor weeks early and there was fear of losing the baby, we ask that You would heal that little one who may also have experienced fear.

"Lord, if the cord was wrapped around the baby's neck; or if because of a long labor, there was a lack of oxygen; or if there was *placenta previa* and grave danger, and the baby almost died at birth, please heal that trauma and emotional wound. If there was no father figure at birth, dear Lord, please give this person the father's love."

In praying for a medical doctor, the Holy Spirit revealed to me that she had almost died at birth. She explained that her mother went into hard, fast labor. All the delivery rooms were filled. The doctors and nurses said for the mother to cross her legs to keep the baby from coming.

[4]Dr. Thomas Verny, *The Secret Life of the Unborn Child* (N.Y. 1981), pp. 20-21.

The Two Steps of Inner Healing

The mother was in the midst of agonizing labor pains. She was in a rage that those around her were keeping the baby from coming naturally.

The Holy Spirit revealed to me that the baby must have felt rejection. "Why don't they want me?" Could it be that the baby felt her mother's rage and anger? Perhaps the baby was wondering, "Is that anger directed towards me?" "Why is there so much anger, fear, and turmoil?" "Why is everyone mad at me?" "Why is my head hurting so much?"

All through the years this doctor has always felt pressure bearing down on her head. I believe this was from the trauma at birth, and she agrees with me. Both the mother and daughter have dealt with anger towards each other all their lives.

I believe it was a big breakthrough when the Holy Spirit revealed the revelation knowledge that it was not anger directed toward each other, but anger and fear that they both felt during that very painful and traumatic birthing process.

SHORTLY AFTER BIRTH

When a baby is given up for adoption, I always ask the person to forgive his or her birth parents at this point in the prayer for healing of memories. *"Can a woman forget her own baby and not love the child she bore? Even if a mother should forget her child, I will never forget you"* (Isaiah 49:15, St. Jerome Bible).

If the parents wanted a boy and the baby was a girl, and they were keenly and bitterly disappointed, that little baby may feel deep rejection and the parents' disappointment, and will need prayer for rejection. Of course, if the baby was abandoned, abused, neglected, or had to stay in the hospital nursery for months because of critical health problems, then that baby will need prayer to be set free from fear and rejection.

If the mother died at birth, there needs to be the breaking of all harmful genetic and emotional soul ties, and also the healing of grief. Ask the Heavenly Father to give a mother's love to the baby. Usually a baby given up for adoption and, in some cases, living in many different foster homes before the final adoption, will have feelings of rejection and insecurity that will need to be healed by our loving Father.

When the baby is one of twins and one baby died, the living baby often will feel guilt for being alive, and grief for the one who died.

While being driven 75 miles to my parents' home in an airport shuttle bus, the driver asked me what I did as a profession.

Hurrah! I love it when that question pops up. I shared with her that I wrote books and held seminars in the U.S. and other countries on inner healing, forgiveness, and the healing of broken hearts.

In the two-hour drive to my parents' home (thank goodness I was the only passenger), I had the privilege of praying with her for inner healing.

She had been a twin; however, her twin had died at birth. The lady was a grown woman but always wondered, "Why do I have such guilt feelings, rejection, and fear? Why do I feel that I don't have a right to live?"

Those feelings went all the way back to her birth, when she experienced her twin's death. My daughter, Tamara, when reading this, said, "She also could have felt added false guilt in growing up when family members may have said (without meaning to bring pain), 'She had a twin, but it died.' "

As I prayed for her for inner healing, she cried and cried — all the while doing an excellent job of driving from the Dallas-Fort Worth Airport for two hours on a freeway. Glory!

She felt an incredible release as the spirits of death, grief, and false guilt were bound and cast from her in the name of Jesus.

PRAYER FOR THE FIRST FIVE YEARS

Pray for each age — one, two, three, four. As the Holy Spirit reveals a vision or Word of Knowledge, stop and pray, asking Jesus to heal. If the child almost died of pneumonia and was in the hospital, ask the Lord to heal that trauma. If family fighting and alcoholism caused fear, rejection, and insecurity, then pray for that wound. Ask the Lord to heal the painful memories.

BEGINNING OF SCHOOL YEARS

Ask the Lord to heal the embarrassments that occurred in elementary school. Many times children are teased, shunned, taunted, bullied, and the school years were times of dread and fear. If a child stuttered, did not have nice clothes to wear, had ears that stuck out, didn't have money for supplies or the extra ten or fifteen cents daily for dessert — all these things brought feelings of embarrassment and not fitting in, of being different and alone. These memories caused pain and need to be healed by Jesus.

An Episcopal priest from a western state shared that when he was born, his mother had a nerve that was accidentally severed which left her paralyzed and in bed.

He could remember, as a first-grader and in later school years, that his first responsibility the moment he got home from school was to go to his mother's room to say hello, and to see if she was okay, or to see if she needed anything.

*This young boy "perceived" this simple request of seeing if his mother needed anything as a request to see **if she were still alive.***

As he walked toward his mother's room, his heart pounded, and he became almost frantic. He was so afraid that he would find her dead. (Every day he would go through this same struggle of fear — "Is she dead? Is she okay? Is she dead?" He was terrified, but yet, he never shared this deep fear with anyone until he was an adult and going through prayer for inner healing.)

This heavy burden as a young child placed much fear in his spirit. In fact, these fears in later years (even as a priest) raised their ugly heads as:

— Fear of failure,

— Fear of people, and

— Fear of marriage and problems with sexual identity.

He had had numerous sessions of inner healing prayer from different counselors. I prayed an in-depth inner healing prayer also. I joined my prayer with others that the root cause of this trauma would be ripped out completely, and that God's healing power would flow and set him completely free.

27

If the child had difficulty learning, or had severe discipline problems, or perhaps was hyperactive and was always in trouble from these experiences, these leave scars also.

". . . Don't keep on scolding and nagging your children, making them angry and resentful. Rather, bring them up with the loving discipline the Lord himself approves, with suggestions and godly advice" (Ephesians 6:4, TLB).

SEXUAL TRAUMA

If a child was fondled, sexually molested, kidnapped, physically or verbally abused, there will be deep wounds, and the child will need to be prayed for with gentleness and compassion. Use extreme caution when you enter into this part of their life. Many times a child will bury the pain, fear, and horror of being treated so tragically. Handle these memories with the utmost professionalism, love, and sensitivity.

Of all experiences, there is none more devastating than child molestation. It leaves the child feeling used, dirty, guilty, afraid, angry, betrayed, and rejected. It completely destroys any future good and normal sexual foundation for the child. There is no greater crime than this.

Many times when the child is threatened by a female or male molester, they are told that if they tell a parent or the authorities, they will be beaten, or even killed. Almost always, they tell the child that they will deny the molestation, or even worse, will say that it was the child's fault (especially if it is a daughter) because they flirted and seduced the molester.

This situation leaves the child feeling helpless. Where do they turn for help? What do they do? They feel trapped and completely betrayed. Many times the memories are pushed into the darkest recesses of the mind. When this happens, it may cause abnormal behavior, the feeling of "what's the use?" It may lead to promiscuity, lesbianism, homosexuality, or a deep fear of and hatred for all men or women, and an inability to trust anyone.

WHEN PARENTS DIVORCE

Almost always with divorce there are feelings of rejection, anger, and guilt. ("What did I do to cause the divorce?") The "child within the adult" may be grieving for having to choose between parents. Usually, there is a deep feeling of loneliness and sorrow. Sometimes depression shows up, even in children, in forms of anger and guilt. A divorce can be as painful as, or more so, than death. It is imperative that the child forgive his mother, dad, and any stepparents. If they cannot at that moment for-

29

give, tell them forgiveness is not a feeling, but an
act of the will. Also ask them, "Why don't you let
Jesus forgive through you?" Then lead them in a
prayer of forgiveness.

JUNIOR AND SENIOR HIGH SCHOOL YEARS

Pray for the junior high and high school years,
for feelings of inadequacy, feeling ugly, awkward,
and dumb. If the person was involved in premarital
sex and had an abortion, there will be much guilt
and shame, even a spirit of murder. If a teenager
was involved in alcohol, drugs, the occult, pornography, stealing, vandalism, or extreme rebellion to
church and parents, then all these things will leave
their mark and traumatic scars. We must ask Jesus
to cleanse and heal those wounds. We must help
the teenagers to know that when they ask for forgiveness, then they are forgiven, and they must
forgive themselves.

There are others who need inner healing. For example, the teenagers who may be model students,
perfect children, but may feel so sad because they
never have any dates, and they don't feel as if they
fit in. They never are part of the "in" group. So
they grow up feeling isolated, always on the outside, hurting, unacceptable, unpopular, lonely, living a life with a "happy mask" on, when, in truth,
their heart is breaking.

This is plowed ground in which the seed of suicide could take root.

"Lord, heal the hurts of teenagers having to move time and time again, and having to finish their senior year thousands of miles away from 'home' and miss graduating with their friends."

THE TWENTIES

I usually pray through these years in this manner:

"Lord, heal all the hurts that occurred when this person was in her twenties.

"Heal the hurt of broken relationships and engagements. Lord, heal the hurt of divorce; or the realization that the person you married was not whom he portrayed himself to be.

"Jesus, heal the hurt of an unhappy and unfulfilling marriage — of not being affirmed, loved deeply, or appreciated. Lord, especially heal the hurt when a mate has an adulterous affair. Let forgiveness and grace abound.

"Lord, heal the pain of losing parents, and of feeling alone and abandoned (even as adults).

"Dear Lord, heal the hurt of miscarriages, or not being able to get pregnant."

At an Episcopal retreat in Florida, God did such a beautiful work of healing a young mother's broken heart.

She had had three tubular pregnancies. The final pregnancy left her, of course, with the inability of ever being pregnant again.

She came to the retreat so terribly depressed, but it was glorious to watch as the Inner Healing Seminar continued during the week and God did His mighty work of restoration and healing in this minister's wife.

On the final day of the retreat, I prayed an in-depth prayer of inner healing.

When I finished, she excitedly said, "Oh, let me share something wonderful! Let me share. God gave me a vision!" Her face was literally shining with the glory of the Lord. With animated gestures and much joy she shared the vision that God had given her.

She said, "I saw Jesus holding my three babies. They all were perfect. And Jesus motioned for me to come to them. In the vision, I was running toward my babies and Jesus. Then, someway, somehow, He motioned for me to get up into His lap too, and there I was — on the lap of Jesus and surrounded by my three babies."

"Oh," she said again, "It was such a wonderful vision."

Everyone in the room rejoiced with her for this precious gift from our Lord. What a miracle-working God He is. And how wonderful it was for our being able to witness this precious miracle. Jesus did something for her that no one else could do. He healed her broken heart by giving her a vision of her three perfect babies. Thank You, Lord, for Your love and compassion.

THE THIRTIES

"Lord, heal the hurts in the thirties. The frustration of the husband not getting good promotions, of not having enough money, of bills piling up and no way of paying them.

"Lord, heal the hurt and rejection of desiring to marry, but not having the right person come along. Heal the pain of seeing all your friends with their new babies and growing families, and having the realization that you probably never will have children.

"Heal the painful memories of having to move across the U.S., away from all family and friends — not once but many, many times.

"Heal the deep wounds and painful memories when (or if) your mate was physically or verbally abusive. Heal the devastation of learning your mate was being unfaithful, was on drugs or involved with pornography. Lord, heal the trauma of living with an alcoholic mate.

"Lord, heal the deep trauma of nervous break-downs, chronic illnesses, or a battle with depression, or thoughts of suicide. For those men and women who are workaholics and make their careers more important than their marriages, I pray that You would heal the hurt and loneliness of their mates.

"Lord, heal the agonizing pain of having an autistic child, or one severely mentally retarded who requires daily and constant care." Your heart breaks a little every day with the unfulfilled dreams you had for your child.

LATER YEARS

I continue praying up to their exact age — forties, fifties, sixties, seventies, or over.

"Lord, sometimes the later years are very painful. If the husband was forced by his company to retire early, there may be a form of grief. Heal the hurt and embarrassment of not being able to get another job. Heal the excruciating pain of the one who suffered a stroke, and cannot speak quite as clearly; heal the frustration and embarrassment.

"Lord, heal the hurts of having grown children move away and their never taking the time to call, write, visit, and say 'I love you,' or 'I appreciate you, Mother and Dad.' Or, to ask you to come visit them.

"Lord, heal the strain and anxiety of those having to live on a Social Security check or meager retirement fund. They seem to become less than a person — only a shell trying to dole out a living. Oh, God, heal those hurts.

"Jesus, please heal the stress and pain that some feel because of their advancing years. Perhaps their health and eyesight have begun to fail, or perhaps they no longer can drive, take care of the yard, or make home repairs. They may have fear of death or they could be completely devastated with grief and lone-liness. Oh, God, please heal all of that woundedness."

During the healing of memories prayer, usually the Holy Spirit will reveal to me a particular age — 4, 10, 14, 57, etc. "What happened at that age?" I will ask, and the counselee will share what happened. Then we ask Jesus to heal that trauma and deep wound.

I always end the prayer for healing of memories by praying for the person to be filled with God's love, joy, and peace, etc., and to receive a complete emotional and physical healing from our Heavenly Father — to receive a good and healthy self-image, and to know completely who they are in Christ Jesus.

The next steps in the counseling session are praying for the infilling of the Holy Spirit and anointing with oil.

SCRIPTURE REFERENCES
FOR THIS CHAPTER

Leviticus 19:31, TLB: *"Do not defile yourselves by consulting mediums and wizards, for I am Jehovah your God."*

Exodus 20:5, KJV: *". . . I the LORD thy God am a jealous God, visiting the iniquity of the fathers upon the children unto the third and fourth generation. . . ."*

Leviticus 18:22, TLB: *"Homosexuality is absolutely forbidden, for it is an enormous sin."*

Psalm 139:16, TLB: *"You made all the delicate, inner parts of my body, and knit them together in my mother's womb. Thank you for making me so wonderfully complex! It is amazing to think about. Your workmanship is marvelous — and how well I know it. You were there while I was being formed in utter seclusion! You saw me before I was born and scheduled each day of my life before I began to breathe. Every day was recorded in your Book!"*

Ephesians 6:4, TLB: *"And now a word to you parents. Don't keep on scolding and nagging your children, making them angry and resentful. Rather, bring them up with the loving discipline the Lord himself approves, with suggestions and godly advice."*

Ephesians 6:12, TLB: *"For we are not fighting against people made of flesh and blood, but against persons without bodies — the evil rulers of the unseen world, those mighty satanic beings and great evil princes of darkness who rule this world; and against huge numbers of wicked spirits in the spirit world."*

CHAPTER THREE

YOUR SPIRITUAL COVERING

"Wisdom and good judgment live together, for wisdom knows where to discover knowledge and understanding" (Proverbs 8:12, TLB).

As a prayer counselor, it is vital to be under a spiritual covering. Especially is this necessary if you are a woman.

What do I mean by a "covering"?

A spiritual covering is one person, or several, a cell group, so to speak, whose function is to be of protection and guidance to you. They serve to offer good advice, support, and encouragement — perhaps even warnings. The Bible says, *"I, Wisdom, give good advice and common sense . . ."* (Proverbs 8:14, TLB). These spiritual coverings should be Spirit-filled Christians, dedicated to prayer and fasting, who are willing to lift you up to the Lord and daily intercede for you.

Your spiritual covering or spiritual director must be a friend, someone who is interested in you and your ministry. They must be held in high regard with man, but more importantly, with *God*.

(Of course, your pastor and church should always be your main spiritual covering.)

If you are married, then it is important that your husband approve of what you are doing in ministry. It is absolutely mandatory that your pastor know and approve of the ministry you are in. If he does not approve, find out why. If he does not believe in Biblical inner healing, then find a church whose pastor does approve and will stand behind a Christ-centered ministry of inner healing.

If your pastor doesn't agree with your being in ministry because your family situation is not in order, then get your *own* family in order first. (I am aware that this is much easier said than done.)

Let me hasten to say, lest I am misunderstood. . . .

There will never be a perfect family. We will never have a perfect spouse, perfect marriage, perfect children, perfect households, or certainly not a perfect US!

I am only saying that even though there may be problems here and there, the overall texture and weave of the tapestry of our lives should be one of divine order and beauty.

When my husband, Ed, was alive, I always went forth to minister with his blessings. We both went forth with our pastor's blessings.

Then, after Ed's death, I made a specific appointment to see Pastor Banning. I wanted to bring him up-to-date on Tapscott Ministries and to let him know what the Lord had me doing. I wanted to know in my heart that I had my pastor's approval and the backing of the church (not financial backing but spiritual backing). I wanted to make certain I was under the protection of my pastor and my church. He assured me that I was!

Never have I felt the need of a covering more than when I went forth to minister in Germany for a month after Ed's death. In the Sunday morning service before I left for Germany, Pastor Banning and several other church pastors anointed me with oil, prayed for me, and sent me forth with their blessings. What a sacred, meaningful, and comforting feeling this gave to me.

There are too many women (and men) "doing their own thing" — bouncing off the wall with false prophecy, out of balance, or in false teaching.

Make certain you have a spiritual covering to call forth from you the spirit of balance, responsibility, credibility, truth, and accountability.

I recall a man from a another state who flew in for counseling. He felt the Lord had given him a ministry in inner healing — especially to women. Even as he said that very first sentence, a "red flag" went up in my spirit.

To make a long story short, the man shared how he would minister to the women in their homes during the day when their husbands were at work.

I asked, "Did you check with your pastor about this? Did you get the husbands' approval to pray for their wives?"

"No!" he responded to each question.

He continued the saga, "Some of the husbands were angry at me. The pastor was angry, and wanted me to stop 'whatever' it was I was doing, he said."

"What did I do wrong?" the man asked. (I thought to myself, "It will take me an hour to tell you.")

With gentleness — but absolute firmness — I started to explain:

"Sir," I said,

1. "You should have, first of all, gone to your pastor and shared the call on your life. You should have told him, 'Pastor, I feel that the Lord has called me to pray with people for inner healing. People are coming to me — I'm not seeking them out.'

2.   "You should have also explained your salvation and your baptism in the Holy Spirit experience. You should have explained the manner in which you were ministering. You should have said, 'Pastor, if you approve of this ministry, is there a place I might pray for these people at the church — a place that's quiet, but not secluded, with perhaps someone nearby as I pray?'

3.   "Sir," I continued, "a man should not be going to a home to minister to the wife (at length and without the husband's knowledge or consent) during the day while her husband is at work."

4.   I concluded, "If a woman needs and asks for ministry, then you should take your wife along, or perhaps other Spirit-filled, godly women to be present."

Most pastors are so unbelievably overworked that if a member of his church truly has a gift of counseling or healing, the pastor will be overjoyed to have the lay person help in the heavy case load of counseling.

A pastor must be able to have the utmost confidence in prayer counselors before entrusting his parishioners to them. He is the Shepherd; these are his sheep, and he does not want any potential wolves harming the sheep.

I consider Pastor Banning as my spiritual covering. But I also have other people that I consider part of the framework of my spiritual covering.

Charles and Frances Hunter, who hold worldwide seminars, are also part of my spiritual covering. Frances prayed for me for the infilling of the Holy Spirit in April of 1972. Ed was the first and only Chairman of the Hunter board. (After his death they were so kind to introduce me as the Honorary Chairman.)

Jim and Lois Wheeless, close friends and pastors of a church a few blocks from my home, have been my prayer warriors and sounding boards. Another intercessor friend is Lawrence, a Spirit-filled minister and brother in the Lord. He has anointed gifts of discernment and prophecy and is a prayer warrior who gives wise counsel compassionately.

Another intercessor is Rev. Bob DeGrandis. He has a worldwide ministry, with whom I have worked in the past in radio, Healing the Whole Person Seminars, as Association of Christian Therapists Regional officers, and in coauthoring books.[1]

Fr. David also helped so much during the trying months after Ed's death. He prayed, encouraged, and usually had a word of prophecy for me, just when I needed a word from the Lord the most.

---

[1]*Forgiveness and Inner Healing,* 1980 (in Spanish, *Perdonar Y Sanidad Interior,* 1981) and *Healing of Self-Image,* 1980, 1986 © Rev. Robert DeGrandis and Betty Tapscott.

I also praise God for all those wonderful and cherished prayer warriors (known and unknown); those within my family and among my friends; my staff, Elizabeth Rincon and Joe Van Cloostere; and all the precious volunteers who pray daily for Tapscott Ministries, for me and for my family. I could not make it without everyone's anointed prayers. However . . .

A word of caution: No one, especially prayer counselors, should be running around seeking a word from God from every "Tom, Dick, and Harry." We are primarily responsible for seeking guidance from the Lord ourselves.

It is imperative (especially in these times) to be safely "within the fold" and protected by the outstretched arms of Jesus. The people whom God sends and we ask to be our spiritual coverings and director will help keep us protected. The Word says in Proverbs 8:33, TLB: *"Listen to my counsel — oh, don't refuse it — and be wise."* It is imperative that we have prayer warriors doing battle for us. I praise God for the mighty and persistent intercessors for Tapscott Ministries.

If you're in ministry, you will be on the front line as Satan's target. My daughter Tamara heard a high Satan priest say on television that he and his Satanists from all over the world were the ones who placed curses on all the well-known Christian television leaders. He stated that the Satanists were responsible for all the confusion, embarrassment, sin, and destruction that was plastered on every news-paper and television for weeks when one of the Christian television programs almost crumbled. Whether the Satanist's statement is true or not we have no way of knowing.

> **We must have spiritual coverings (our church or other ministries) a spiritual director and intercessors (our pastor and others) for our spiritual protection and guidance. As prayer counselors in this day and age we need this shield of safety more than ever before.**

CHAPTER FOUR

CARDINAL RULES
(IN MINISTERING INNER HEALING BIBLICALLY)

". . . Don't ever forget that it is best to listen much, speak little . . . and remember . . . to obey, not just to listen . . ." (James 1:19, 22, TLB).

When we hear the word "rules," many times the *child* within us rebels. Nevertheless, there are three cardinal rules in ministering inner healing: (1) Listen to the Holy Spirit; (2) Obey the Holy Spirit; (3) Trust the Holy Spirit.

LISTEN TO THE HOLY SPIRIT

Four years before my husband, Ed's, death, we ministered in England for three weeks. After we finished our speaking tour, we rested for two days at the beautiful Catholic Retreat Center where Fr. Bob DeGrandis was holding a seminar.

The day we arrived, he had just given a talk on resting in the Spirit. Then he announced to the

50-60 psychiatrists, doctors, nurses, priests, and nuns from all over England, "I want you to experience what I've just told you about." He had the entire group make a huge circle. Then he made the sign of the cross on each person's forehead and anointed them with oil. I prayed with Fr. Bob, and Ed caught the people as they rested in the Spirit.

When a priest would start to get up off the floor, Fr. Bob would say, "Bless him again, Lord," and back down the priest would go! The entire group was resting in the Spirit at one time for a long period of time. The power of the Lord was incredible. What a glorious sight!

The Lord brought to my attention a nun, resting in the Spirit. The Lord said, "Go and minister to her." I walked across the room and knelt down by her and started to pray *silently*. Remember now, she was *"resting in the Spirit," and I was praying silently.*

The Lord gave me a Word of Knowledge that she had fear of death and fear of choking. He revealed that the fear had entered at birth. So I prayed silently, *"Lord Jesus, please set her free from this fear, and please heal the traumatic memory of the painful birth, when the umbilical cord was wrapped around her neck."*

Strange as it sounds, as I was praying about the cord being wrapped around her neck, a bright, vivid, red band appeared on her neck. I continued praying, *"Lord, during the long hours of labor, please remove the memory of the pain.''* And even though I was praying silently and she was still resting in the Spirit, she reached up with her hands and grabbed her head, as if she were in pain.

When she got up, I asked the Sister, "What do you know about your birth?" She replied, "Oh! My mum said it was a sixteen-hour, hard and long labor, that the cord was wrapped around my neck, and that I almost died."

"Oh!" she continued, "I feel great. I don't know what happened, but I feel just great."

Two weeks after we arrived back in Houston, I received a letter from this precious nun. She wrote that she had always had such a fear of not being able to breathe that she carried an inhaler in her purse at all times. She said, "I've thrown that away; all the fear is gone."

She continued in her letter, "I've always had such a fear of my fellow nuns. I know they love me and I love them, but I was afraid of not measuring up. Also, I was terrified of speaking in front of groups. Well," she added, "all that fear is gone, too. I spoke twice in one week on inner healing." Praise the Lord!

So, we absolutely must trust the Holy Spirit in ministry. The nun had not shared with me her problem. *I trusted the voice of the Holy Spirit and not my own understanding, and He revealed to me the root cause of her problems.*

OBEY THE HOLY SPIRIT

Ed, my husband, received a phone call one day from three young men at the Houston Greyhound Bus Station. One of the boys said, "I've read Betty's book on inner healing and I asked two of my friends to bring me down from Canada for ministry." He added, "I'm so suicidal I was afraid to come alone."

We had not expected the boys, did not know them, and, unfortunately, they arrived when our schedule was absolutely crammed. We could not even find a moment to minister to them for two days. Finally, on the third day, we were able to minister in-depth to all three. *And* they all three received beautiful miracles from the Lord. Kevin was set free from suicide; one boy gave up drugs and went back to school; and one boy went into a religious order.

Two or three years after this experience, early one Monday morning I heard the Lord say, "Call Kevin! Call Kevin!" I couldn't even remember Kevin's last name, much less his address or phone number. I thought, "Lord, how am I going to call him? I don't know how to reach him."

You can imagine my utter amazement when I walked to my desk that morning, put my things down, and there was a three-year-old letter from Kevin sticking out from under a folder on my desk. It absolutely took my breath away — and I looked around to catch a glimpse of the *angel* who had put it there. Of course, Kevin's phone number was on the bottom of his letter.

I picked the receiver up and dialed. A young man answered. I said, "Is this Kevin?"

"Yes, it is," he replied.

"Kevin, this is Betty Tapscott in Houston. The Lord told me to call you this morning. Are you okay?"

"Oh! Mrs. Tapscott," he said. "My mother died."

"I'm so sorry, Kevin. When did she die?" I asked sympathetically.

"Mrs. Tapscott, she just died. The funeral director hasn't even gotten here yet."

I was stunned.

Kevin continued, "Mrs. Tapscott, God does care about me, doesn't He? He does know I'm hurting, doesn't He? He had you call me so I would know that He really does love and care about me."

"Yes, Kevin, He does," I replied assuredly.

After praying with Kevin, I finished the phone call and hung up the receiver. I leaned back in my chair, took a deep breath, and thought, "Oh! Dear Lord, thank You for having me call when I did. May I always hear Your voice. May I always be IMMEDIATELY OBEDIENT to Your voice."

TRUST THE HOLY SPIRIT

We don't always see the evidence of our prayers being answered immediately. That is when TRUST comes in.

I had just finished speaking to and praying for a ladies group at Braeswood Church in Houston. Eleanore, one of the church secretaries, stopped by to say "hi" and to ask for prayer. When I started praying for her, the Lord seemed to say that she had one arm shorter than the other. Indeed she did, and as we prayed the Lord lengthened it. I also felt that there was something very traumatic that had happened to her which she wasn't sharing. When I questioned her, she kept saying, "No, everything is okay. I'm just fine."

When I got home, the phone rang and it was Eleanore. "Mrs. Tapscott, there *is* something wrong. I have M.S. (multiple sclerosis). No one knows about it here at church." She continued to share, "As you were praying earlier this morning, it felt as if electricity was going through my body." She excitedly said, "I believe God is healing me of M.S. Please, can we pray some more?"

And we did! I, too, felt a heavy anointing from the Lord. Eleanore said that her entire body was burning with heat and that she was tingling all over.

We finally finished praying, and she shared later (at a Healing the Whole Person Seminar with Fr.

DeGrandis and myself) that she didn't want to let go of the receiver, because she was afraid the power of the Lord would stop.

Praise the Lord! All the M.S. symptoms were gone. Some time later she had to go into the hospital for another problem. When the doctor saw her huge chart on M.S., he said, "Let's run some new tests." He didn't quite believe Eleanore when she said, "The Lord has healed me." When the tests for M.S. were run, however, there was proof. No M.S.! She had been miraculously healed by our precious Lord Jesus Christ.

So even though we may not see immediate results, we must always remember to TRUST THE HOLY SPIRIT.

CHAPTER FIVE

PRAYER COUNSELORS

"Share each others troubles and problems"
(Galatians 6:2, TLB).

*". . . the wisdom that comes from heaven is first
of all pure and full of quiet gentleness. . . . It is
peace-loving and courteous. It allows discussion
and is willing to yield to others; it is full of mercy
and good deeds. It is wholehearted and straight-
forward and sincere. And those who are peace-
makers will plant seeds of peace and reap a
harvest of goodness"* (James 3:17-18, TLB).

WE MINISTER WHAT WE ARE

We can never be perfect. In fact, Fr. Henri
Nouwen says that we are all "wounded healers."
However, we, as ministers, must keep our temples
clean and the channels open in order that God's
healing power can flow through us.

LEAVE THE RESULTS TO GOD

If the person you pray for is healed . . . God did it. If they are not healed . . . that is in God's hands also. As counselors (even PRAYER COUNSELORS) we cannot heal anyone. We are not a magic button to push. We must leave the results to God, and give Him all praise and glory.

SHOULD YOU EVER SAY "NO" WHEN SOMEONE ASKS FOR IN-DEPTH MINISTRY?

One of the hardest things to do is to say "no" to someone when they ask for ministry. "Why would anyone want to say no?" you might ask. Because we may not be the person God has planned to pray for them; He may have especially anointed another person to pray. It may not be God's timing to pray. The person may not be repentant and ready to give up his sin (if that is the problem).

Another reason to say NO is this: If a person calls and calls and calls for prayer and never seems to be helped, you may hear the Lord say for you to tell the person, "Obviously my prayers are not ministering to you. I believe you need to ask someone else to pray for you."

We seem to think that if WE don't pray for someone, they won't get healed. That just isn't so!

53

There may come a time in the course of ministering that you will have to say to the person: "I cannot pray with *you* any more. I have done all I can, God has done His part, and until you do your part, please do not ask for any more prayer." (Assure the person that you will still be praying *FOR* them — just not *WITH* them.)

For example . . .

Several years ago a lady from a midwestern state would call the ministry two to three times a day for prayer. Then it was only two to three times a week. Always I or the staff would say in the course of the conversation,

"Are you reading your Bible?"

"No!" was her answer.

"Are you going to church?"

"No!"

"Are you going to a prayer fellowship?"

"No!"

"Have you found a prayer partner yet?"

"No!"

"Are you praying in English and in the Spirit?"

"No!"

"Are you praising God?"

54

"No — I can't."

This identical conversation went on for weeks and months. We prayed, and prayed, and prayed. She would get victory, but then she would not do the things required to keep her healing.

Then, I heard the Lord say, "Tell her you cannot pray for her any more until she does some of the things that you've suggested to help her grow in the Spirit." I know spiritual growth takes time and patience. It is a continuing process and not usually achieved overnight. However, there must be true repentance, self-control, and a desire to live for the Lord in complete obedience.

Finally, one day I firmly, but with love, told her, "Do not call back any more until you start doing at least some of the things I've asked you to." When I said this, I looked over to see a most shocked look on the face of Joe, my office manager.

But it worked. A few months later, she called back to say that she realized that what I had told her was true, and that she had to start trying to help herself and not depend on a "magic button" in the form of a minister or ministry to set her free.

"Betty, you were right," she said. "God did His part. You did your part, but I had to do my part also."

YOU MAY HAVE TO HAVE THE FAITH
FOR SOMEONE

On the other hand, you as a mature, Spirit-filled counselor may have *to have the faith for a broken-hearted person* with a horribly crushed and wounded spirit. You may need to take her hand and gently say, "My friend, I'm going to walk through this valley with you. Don't be afraid."

THE PRAYER TEAMS

I rejoiced when I heard Rita Bennett say at a seminar in Houston that all those on prayer teams should be silent during the time of ministry and that ONLY ONE PERSON SHOULD BE VERBAL. Hurrah for you, Rita! This is so important — and you're right on target!

It is hard for a person being prayed for to concentrate on several people at the same time. It is hard, also, for the one counseling if others keep breaking in, changing the flow and direction of the session. It is especially difficult if some of the prayer team members are not anointed in the gifts and keep calling out invalid Words of Knowledge.

I find it very difficult myself to counsel or pray for someone when other people are praying loudly in the Spirit (or even quietly), or interjecting their own views. It's disconcerting to me, and I am used to praying in the Spirit and hearing people pray out loud in their prayer language.

Think what it must be like to a nervous counselee subjected to this: six voices praying loudly all at once, while the counselor is trying to pray quietly with the person. It would be difficult for the counselee, as well as the counselor. So, you wonderful prayer teams, please pray SILENTLY and do not interrupt unless asked to do so by the one leading the ministering.

How would you feel if you went to a doctor and there were several nurses or interns speaking all at once, and each one had a different opinion of what was wrong with you?

And yet this is what we do when we subject a person to several people sitting around him, all praying in the Spirit, or all talking at the same time. I don't know about you, but I would not want to be ministered to in that fashion.

BE CAUTIOUS ABOUT PRAYING ALONE WITH THE OPPOSITE SEX

Unless you are a licensed professional counselor, it is better for a woman to pray with a woman, and a man with a man, unless you have someone with you. Of course, there are always those times of exceptions, but it should be the *exception* and not general practice.

Obviously a professional counselor will minister alone in his or her office with the secretary right outside the door at her desk.

It is certainly wise not to minister alone, however, with the opposite sex in motel rooms (after conferences), in secluded and locked church offices, or even in the privacy of your own home. (I don't care how spiritual you are.)

I recall a man, years ago, wanting counseling in my pre-office and staff days. I said, "You must bring your wife with you." He agreed, but arrived the next day without his wife, looking very dapper and handsome.

"Sir," I said, "I'm sorry, but I will not minister to you without your wife." I said a quick prayer at the door. The man left, and he and his wife came back the next day.

The wife had been pleasantly surprised. It seemed that her husband had a roving eye for women and when he had announced, "I'm going to have this lady pray with me for inner healing at her home," her first reaction was one of doubt and suspicion.

I ended up by ministering to this entire family and saw them all filled with the Holy Spirit — only because I used caution in not praying for the man in my house alone.

JUST YOU, GOD AND THE OTHER PERSON

There may be times, however, in an emergency counseling session, when it is just *you, the person you're praying for, and of course, God!* And always with the presence of the Father, Son and Holy Ghost, that makes a majority.

If a child were drowning, we women, even if alone, would throw in the life ring, and jump into the pool to rescue the child, without a life guard license or without someone there to help us. Likewise, there are times of emergency prayer sessions when we have to pray deliverance alone.

For example . . .

Ed and I had just attended an international conference where one of the speakers spoke on deliverance. In his talk, the man made it very clear that he felt women should never — absolutely NEVER pray for deliverance.

I sensed a spiritual pride and egotism in this person, and had to pray for my own attitude towards his chauvinistic spirit.

After the conference, I flew on to California to speak to a church and appear on television, while Ed flew back to Houston. In a few days I finished my meetings and obligations and was preparing to leave for the airport to fly back to Houston also.

The lady who was to take me to the airport brought her grown niece with her saying, "Betty, would you say a quick blessing prayer for her before we dash off to the airport?" Of course, I would.

We sat down on the edge of the motel bed and I started praying. I quickly discerned a spirit of self-hate and said, "I bind the spirit of self-hate in the name of Jesus."

The young woman instantly started manifesting strange demonic behavior. Her face turned red as an apple. The veins on her neck protruded to gigantic size. She was trying to scream (but in the name of Jesus I was binding that unholy spirit to silence). Her hands and fingers were moving in a grotesque and inhuman manner and position.

I looked over at my precious friend Diane — her eyes were big as saucers. She asked, "What do I do?"

"Just pray in the Spirit," I said.

A funny thought dashed through my mind. I chuckled to myself. The conference speaker had said, "No woman should ever pray for deliverance." Ed was back in Houston and here I was in a motel room with a woman sent by God and obviously in need of deliverance! Oh! Glory! Pray I must, and be obedient to my Heavenly Father — whether the conference speaker agreed or not!

I felt the peace, power, protection, and anointing of the Holy Spirit. I prayed for ministering angels to be all around. I prayed that we all would be covered symbolically in the shed blood of Jesus. God had sent this young woman to me for prayer and I was going to pray with her!

I can't say, "Now, to make a long story short . . ." because it wasn't a long story. I only had a few moments to pray before leaving to catch my plane. But to put the experience in a nutshell: The lady was throwing up green slime (her head was in the toilet bowl, almost touching the water). She was barking like a dog and growling.

But — praise the Lord! The bondage was completely broken! The chains were broken. The Word says, *"For God will break the chains that bind his people and the whip that scourges them . . ."* (Isaiah 9:4, TLB).

She was beautifully set free, delivered, healed, and transformed in just a few minutes. Let me hasten to say that inner healing usually takes much longer than this. It usually is a process. There's usually not an instantaneous miracle, such as this one. But, praise God for this one.

We all three laughed and I said, "Well, the Lord knew I had to catch that plane." And, after all, God is the One who breaks the yoke — it is His anointing. I was just the fortunate one who happened to be there to pray inner healing for her. And because of God's generosity, grace, and His wanting to *bless me* as well as *heal her,* I was able to see a glorious miracle performed right before my eyes.

I was back in California the next year to hold another inner healing seminar. Before the church service started, a beautiful, serene-looking young woman was pointed out to me in the crowd.

"Do you recognize her?" my friend asked.

"No, I don't think so," I responded.

"That's my niece whom you prayed deliverance for last year at the motel. You remember you only had fifteen minutes before we had to leave to go to the airport?"

It all came back to me. "Yes, of course, I remember," I said. "How could I forget?"

Diane said, "Betty, my niece now prays for others for inner healing." Praise the Lord!

BE CONFIDENT ENOUGH TO SAY: "YOU NEED PROFESSIONAL HELP."

— You may need to see a PHYSICIAN.

It may be clogged arteries and a closed heart valve instead of a broken heart causing those chest pains. You may be depressed because of a chemical or hormonal imbalance. Of course, God heals! However, we cannot manipulate Him, and He may want to heal you through medicine or surgery. I praise God for the following words:

"Give doctors the honor they deserve, for the Lord gave them their work to do. Their skill came from the Most High. . . . The Lord created medicines from the earth, and a sensible person will not hesitate to use them. . . . He gave medical knowledge to human beings, so that we would praise him for the miracles he performs. The druggist mixes these medicines, and the doctor will use them to cure diseases and ease pain. There is no end to the activities of the Lord, who gives health to the people of the world.

"Son, when you get sick, don't ignore it. Pray to the Lord, and he will make you well. Confess all your sins and determine that in the future you will live a righteous life. . . . Then call the doctor — for the Lord created him — and keep him at your side; you need him. There are times when you have to depend on his skill. The doctor's prayer is that the Lord will make him able to ease his patients' pain and make them well again" (Sirach 38:1-14, St. Jerome).

— You may need to see a Christian PSYCHOLO-GIST or PSYCHIATRIST.

Even after inner healing prayer, there may still be such deep-seated problems that the person will need in-depth testing and long-term counseling.

We need to know when we are dealing with: an anorexic, a manic depressive, a psychopath, a schizophrenic, etc. These people are not out of

God's capability to heal, however, often they are out of the lay counselor's realm of competency to help. The anorexic may be so dehydrated and physically ill that she needs to be hospitalized for forced feedings.

We are not limiting God. We are simply recognizing our own limitations and realizing that the person not only needs prayer counseling, but perhaps medication, even hospitalization, as well as long-term professional counseling and reprogramming.

> **If a person is threatening suicide, he or she should be referred to a Christian psychiatrist, immediately. Certainly, the pastor should know the severity of the situation concerning his church member.**

— You may need to see a NUTRITIONIST.

A doctor of preventive medicine or a nutritionist will encourage you to get off colas and all cold drinks that are fizzy; to eliminate coffee, tea, cigarettes, alcohol, chocolate, and especially sugar. Many nutritionists even say to eliminate all white foods (sugar, salt, white flour, shortening, pasta, rice) from your diet. They will also say to get off all junk food. (Did I hear a moan?) It is so important to eat fresh fruits, vegetables, fish, chicken, and very little meat. Pray for the Lord's wisdom and always check with your doctor before starting on any stringent diet or long-term fasting.

I recently heard two people (one a Ph.D. specializing in nutrition, and the other an M.D. in internal medicine and specializing in nutrition and preventive medicine) say, "Just eliminating sugar from diets can set many people free from depression or disease."

We can't live on donuts and coffee for breakfast, and colas and chips for lunch, and expect to feel physically, emotionally, or spiritually vibrant day after day. I don't believe God will heal as long as we deliberately abuse our body. (I'm talking to myself also. I tend to go "90 miles an hour" without proper rest or meal breaks.)

I was blessed when I read this: *". . . as you go through life, keep your appetite under control, and don't eat anything that you know is bad for you. All food doesn't agree with everyone, and everyone doesn't like the same kinds of food. Don't feel you just have to have all sorts of fancy food, and don't be a glutton over any food. If you eat too much, you'll get sick; if you do it all the time, you'll always have stomach trouble. Gluttony has been the death of many people. Avoid it and live longer"* (Sirach 37:27-31, St. Jerome).

— You may need to join an EXERCISE PRO-GRAM.

If we cannot discipline ourselves to walk at least one mile every day, then our body will continue to sag, droop, and we will constantly be plagued by fatigue. (I made sure I walked my mile this morning before I wrote this — I must be more diligent, however, in exercising.)

It is a wonderful time to pray in the Spirit when you are taking a walk by yourself. I return home physically and spiritually refreshed.

MAKE CERTAIN THAT YOU HAVE A SPIRITUAL COVERING

I have already mentioned the importance of a covering. But I'm reminded of the tragic case of the woman who was creating all sorts of problems in every church that she was in. A pastor called one day asking me to please pray for some young women in his church.

They had been involved in a "prayer group" led by Mrs. "X," and had gotten so confused. They all were now having strife at home and many other problems. The pastor continued, "This came about since the beginning of their relationship with Mrs. 'X.' " The pastor finally had to ask the lady to leave his church.

Soon a pastor from another church called: "Betty, would you please pray for some women in my church? A particular woman has come to my church and has created havoc." It was the same story as before. The pastor said, "I didn't want to, but I had to ask her to leave."

Soon, even another pastor called, "Betty, one of my church members has recently become entangled in the web of false teaching by a new lady in my church. Would you pray for my church member, please, as a personal favor?"

The woman in question did not have any spiritual coverings; neither the spiritual covering of a church, nor the spiritual covering of her husband. No wonder she was "bouncing off the wall" creating havoc, dissension, and deception everywhere she went. It is a very tragic story indeed. WE MUST HAVE SPIRITUAL COVERINGS!

WILL YOU "LIKE" EVERYONE YOU PRAY WITH?

NO, you may not *like* everyone that you pray with, but we will *love* them because the Word says, *"Beloved, let us love one another: for love is of God; and every one that loveth is born of God, and knoweth God"* (1 John 4:7, KJV).

Some of the people who come to you may be arrogant, antagonistic, cynical, filled with self-pity, unkempt, or filled with spiritual pride. Some may be homosexuals with AIDS. Some people are not willing to listen or take advice. Some have absolutely no self-control or self-discipline. They want to blame ALL of their present problems on the past. They can't believe that any part of their problem could be caused by their own doing. Some may be spiritual leeches, constantly going from one counselor, ministry, church, or pastor to another.

When someone like this comes, what do you do? I ask forgiveness of my own negative emotions, and as a prayer counselor, I then try to find the root cause of their problems and try to see the person as Jesus sees them — a child of the King, a joint-heir with Jesus Christ, the apple of His eye, and a person for whom Jesus died.

We need to pray for the Lord to fill us with His love and compassion and really know that sitting before us is one of God's wounded children. We need to pray for the grace to look over and beyond their problems and see them the way God made them to be. We don't have to *like* what they are, or what they do, but God would have us to *love* them. His Word says, *"Love your neighbor as yourself"* (see Matthew 19:19, KJV).

CHAPTER SIX

THE COMPASSIONATE PRAYER

In quoting Charles Hunter: "Not all are 'called' to minister inner healing, and not all are qualified. Seek your pastor's counsel if you have a desire to minister inner healing. Are you using all the Gifts God has given you? Do you have the ability to use the Gifts, Word of Knowledge or Gift of Discerning of Spirits? If not, ministering inner healing is not for you."

We Must Never Allow Our Prayers to Injure an Already Wounded Person

1. We must never pray in a manner where the counselee walks away after we've prayed with them with even more of a heaviness of heart and a "bad taste in their mouth" because of our thoughtless or insensitive prayers.

2. We must never pray something intentionally and deliberately, knowing that our comments would sting. Our inappropriate prayer would be an "angry" prayer, a judgmental prayer. *The person would wish that you hadn't prayed at all.*

3. Sometimes people are inclined to say things in a prayer that they would never say to the person in a natural conversation. This is like in needling or teasing; they are saying what they truly feel from the negativity that is in their heart, but in this situation their words tumble out as a prayer. This is a resentful and unloving action and should not be called prayer at all.

4. Some prayers are similar to a small tornado; a whirl of dust, a lot of noise: result — destruction and debris. Some people, as they pray, verbalize their inner feelings with this type of prayer: if the prayer hits a need or request, okay; if it doesn't, the one who prays is not the least bit concerned. They may pray around the world with much gusto, and worn religious cliches, but without ever praying specifically for the needs or requests mentioned.

5. Some prayers hurt by trying to make the person feel inept, guilty, inadequate, a worrier, or filled with fear and nervousness. These types of prayers (and we probably all have had them prayed over us) are "put down" prayers. They are negative and unaffirming. I trust that we

have never "prayed" them as prayer counselors ourselves.

6. Then, there are some who pray their *own needs,* instead of *your needs* in their prayers. For example:

    A friend was prayed with for the healing of her womb and ovaries. She had a hysterectomy many years ago. Actually the person praying was concerned about her own upcoming surgery.

    I had a person pray one time, "Oh, dear Lord, help Betty find quiet time today." As it was, I'd been up every morning that week at three o'clock to pray in my prayer room. Later, she commented, "I never can find the time to pray."

7. There are those who pray "canned" prayers; short, curt, memorized; the same phrases each time. If we do this, we are not praying the Mind of Christ. We are in a spiritual rut. Unfortunately, some phone ministry prayers are occasionally like this.

Oh, dear Lord, forgive us each one for any time we have vandalized Your beautiful gift — prayer.

WHAT KIND OF PRAYERS
SHOULD WE PRAY?

— Prayers with sincerity and saturated with the love of Jesus.

— Prayers that are as specific as possible.

— Prayers that are adorned with compassion and sensitivity.

— Prayers that encourage and help to revive visions, and that instill faith.

— Prayers that lift each person up to Jesus.

— Prayers that liberate and heal.

— Prayers that are in line with the Mind of Christ.

— Prayers that can be backed up with the Word of God. In fact, we should PRAY THE WORD.

WHAT TYPE OF PRAYER DO YOU WANT?

When I am hurting, discouraged, in physical pain, or overwhelmed with grief; when I've failed at something; or when I'm just extremely weary:

I would want someone to pray for me as if they were pleased to pray for me, and that it was not an imposition at all, and as if they had a surplus of time to do so.

I would want someone to pray sincerely and specifically for my particular problems.

I would want someone to correct me if need be, but gently and with love; certainly without a "holier-than-thou" or a "put-down" attitude.

I would like someone to encourage me, instill faith in me, remind me of any good points (we all do have some, you know).

I would enjoy someone using a gentle sense of humor in their prayers, if it is warranted. (Jesus was not only a loving Jesus but a laughing Jesus.)

I would like to have someone bind and cast out any unholy spirit and pray for any painful memories that I might have.

I would want them to tell me how much God loves me, and to pray with the love and compassion of Jesus for me.

WHEN YOU'VE BEEN PRAYED FOR IN THIS MANNER:

— Usually your pain is gone.

— The oppression is lifted.

— Your confusion is gone and you have new direction.

— All negativity and tension is bound from you.

— A song is loosed within your heart.

— Your faith is lifted up. You are encouraged and blessed. There is peace within your heart.

> **When you are prayed for with the compassion of Jesus, and the anointed gifts from the Holy Spirit, your wounded spirit will have the healing ointment of the Holy Spirit poured on it with the sweet fragrance of Jesus. His peace, His hope, and His *unconditional love* will permeate your very being, and you will be able to say, "It is well with my soul."**

If on those rare occasions, you did not *feel anything* after being prayed for (no warm feeling, no goose bumps, no lifting of your spirit, no freedom from pain), you can still know that when you were taken into the presence of Jesus you received a touch from Him either spiritually, physically, or emotionally.

Whether you "feel" it or not, *every* prayer helps, every prayer is heard, and we can truly say, "He touched me, oh, He touched me."

CHAPTER SEVEN

B.L.T. — PLEASE

"Do your best to present yourself to God as one approved, a workman who does not need to be ashamed and who correctly handles the word of truth" (2 Timothy 2:15, NIV). *(Balance)*

". . . let us practice loving each other, for love comes from God and those who are loving and kind show that they are the children of God" (1 John 4:7, TLB). *(Love)*

"Jesus said to them, 'You are truly my disciples if you live as I tell you to, and you will know the truth, and the truth will set you free' " (John 8:31b-32, TLB). *(Truth)*

What do I mean by B.L.T.? Bacon-lettuce-tomato sandwich? Basic-Leadership-Training? No! I mean:

BALANCE
LOVE
TRUTH

"What does this have to do with ministering inner healing biblically?" you may ask. Absolutely everything — because . . .

We are to minister inner healing in Balance, Love, and Truth! (B.L.T.) This is the Christ-centered way!

Whether we are involved in teaching, preaching, prayer counseling, writing, or ministering inner healing — every word, action, or deed must be done with: Balance, Love, and Truth.

BALANCE

In the last few years, unfortunately, many churches or ministries have gone off-center, or way out of balance in their doctrines, teachings, and beliefs. This has caused confusion and dissension in the Body of Christ.

Perhaps the "mother" churches, original ministries, or Bible schools were in balance. It could be that only some of the members or students became out-of-balance. We may have read about, been a member of, or perhaps only a follower-from-afar of a ministry or church that has tragically gone into error and swung out of balance. When this happens, it brings pain and discredit to the entire Body of Christ.

Our main goal and concern in ministering must always be one of BALANCE! We should make this our daily prayer.

B.T.L. — Please

Prayer for Balance

Dear Lord, please keep me in Balance. Help me always to use the common sense and wisdom that You gave me. Lord, please give me seeing eyes and hearing ears to those things in the Spirit. And Lord, increase daily Your Gifts of Discernment, Wisdom, and Word of Knowledge in my life. Lord, always keep me grounded in You. Thank You for keeping me in Balance. In Jesus' name. Amen.

LOVE

No matter how anointed the minister or counselor, if there is no love of Jesus evident in their lives, no fruit of the Spirit displayed, then something is wrong.

Some time ago I was blessed by a sermon. I wanted to briefly tell the visiting evangelist how much his message touched my heart. When I approached the pulpit, he was so unfriendly and rude, that I was really sorry I had taken the time to thank him. But, even though his attitude wasn't a blessing, his sermon was.

And would you believe that many people have come for prayer for inner healing because they had been previously wounded by, *of all people,* another counselor, pastor, or visiting evangelist, the very ones that God called upon to help people.

77

I recall a Canadian lady in a wheelchair who had been embarrassed and emotionally wounded the week before. She was told by an evangelist that if she only had enough FAITH, she would be healed. As she shared this hurt with me, tears ran from her eyes.

I glanced down at her legs. They were "match stems," left that way when she was four years of age and had a ravaging bout with polio. The visiting evangelist left her wounded in spirit by his lack of love and compassion. She said, "Don't pray for physical healing or a creative miracle, but please pray for my wounded spirit."

We must always minister in compassion, gentleness, patience, and most of all, His boundless and unconditional LOVE.

Our Prayer to Be Filled With God's Love

Dear Lord, Your Word tells us to love our neighbor as ourselves. Father, in the name of Jesus, I ask that You fill me to overflowing with Your divine love. Help me to love the unloving, the unlovely, and those who will not love me in return.

Jesus, may Your love saturate my entire being. May my eyes sparkle with Your love. May my face shine with Your Shekinah glory and Your love.

May my voice project gentleness and Your love. May my actions line up with Your words, "Love one another." *Thank You, Lord, for helping me to love myself (as You do), to love others, and to be open to receive Your love. Help me to love all those around me with Your love, so they will see You in me. In the name of Jesus. Amen.*

TRUTH

With so many people dabbling in Humanism, New Age, or Mind Sciences, some of it is bound to carry over into our churches. We MUST — ABSOLUTELY MUST base all of our ministering, teaching, preaching, and counseling on *Jesus Christ.*

> **Our prayer counseling for inner healing must be Bible-oriented counseling. Our prayer counseling must be Christ-centered! It must be based on the shed blood of Jesus Christ. It must be based on GOD'S TRUTH.**

In traveling across the U.S. and into other countries, I have heard of some ministering in inner healing being done that did not portray or stand for the things of the Lord — for example, Truth.

The ministry had been diluted, fragmented, and diverted from God's truth. The person may include some transcendental meditation, some yoga, a little of this, or a little of that. They may include just enough truth to sound okay. However, they also may include just enough error to be dangerous and a threat to discredit the valid, God-centered ministries of inner healing.

Ministering in Truth means that we're not going to be "Granola Christians" (made up of flakes, nuts, and fruit). But that we are going to be grounded in the Word, filled with His power, using common sense, wisdom, and our intellect, walking the walk, and talking the talk of *Truth.* Anyone counseling or operating in the gifts of the Spirit should spend "much" time in the Bible to know the truth. To know that *"if the Son sets you free, you will indeed be free"* (John 8:36, TLB).

Our Prayer for Truth

Dear Lord, please don't let me ever go into error. Keep Your ministering and guardian angels around me. Protect me by Your Holy Spirit. May I always walk in Your light and never in darkness. Keep me safe from any deceiving spirit. May I always share Your TRUTH in boldness, with a pure countenance and a wholesome transparency.

Lord, I pray that You will give me wisdom, knowledge, and discernment. May I always hear Your voice. Teach me Your truths, dear Lord, and may I always walk in that path of TRUTH. In Jesus' name. Amen.

CHAPTER EIGHT

MINISTERING DO'S

"Heal the sick, raise the dead, cure the lepers, and cast out demons. Give as freely as you have received!" (Matthew 10:8, TLB).

1. DO SHOW LOVE

Agape love is healing. A gentle, Christlike touch is soothing. The person we are praying for must see this Jesus love and compassion in us.

In some churches a particular message is strongly adhered to and is so out-of-balance! A person cannot be open, honest, nor express his true feelings of: "I'm hurting. I'm grieving. I'm lonely. I'm depressed. Please help me; I need help! Please love me; console me. My spirit is wounded and broken."

A man in another city had been driving his car when he had an accident. It killed his three-year-old child and pregnant wife. The accident had been caused by his own judgment error. The church he was attending espoused, "absolutely no negative confession." Consequently, this poor broken-hearted husband and father could not talk to anyone about his overwhelming grief and guilt. As Spirit-filled Christians, we must not be legalistic and unbending.

We must listen with the ears of Jesus and show His unconditional love.

2. DO RADIATE JOY

Not a flippant "Just praise the Lord now!" But sincere, contagious joy and peace. Perhaps even a precious, and timely sense of humor.[1] One of my favorite pictures of Jesus is called the "Laughing Jesus."

However, we must always be so attuned to the Spirit that when He would have us hold a mother's hand as she shares the heartache of having just lost a child through miscarriage, we would feel free to cry with her, to put our arm around her shoulder, and be free to show the compassionate love of Jesus to her.

[1]Cheryl, who was my secretary for several years, has such a warm sense of humor. It is gentle, always in good taste. It is never used as teasing, but it is a gift from God that blesses people and relieves tension. Her sense of humor brings hope, and warms hearts (not to mention "keeping you in stitches" laughing). *"A cheerful heart does good like medicine . . ."* (Proverbs 17:22, TLB).

What I'm trying to say is . . .

We, as counselors, must never be stern, impatient, cold-hearted, or a "pious know-it-all." You, as a counselor, will bring a certain measure of healing just by your warmth and joy and by the radiance and Shekinah Glory of the Jesus who lives in you.

3. DO BE GENTLE

We choose a dentist by his reputation for gentleness, right? Is it any less important that we be known for our own gentle spirit as we minister inner healing to the broken and bruised Body of Christ?

Emotional wounds are painful. They may be raw, sore, bleeding, or raging with infection. Sharing the secret sin of an abortion, for example, is devastating. Recently a grandmother revealed her 47-year-old secret of abortion. She said the guilt was "killing" her. She was overwhelmed by grief and guilt. Through a Word of Knowledge, God set her free and healed her. Praise the Lord! The ministry to her had to be with the grace, mercy, love, and forgiveness of our precious Lord.

Sharing the shame of child molestation can be agonizingly embarrassing and traumatic to the victim. We, as counselors, must be gentle. That deeply embedded thorn must come out of the wound before the person can be healed. The swollen abscess must be lanced before emotional healing can take place. ALL THIS REQUIRES GENTLENESS.

How would we want to be ministered to? With gentleness and compassion.

When a child falls off his tricycle, we don't say, "Serves you right!" Adults can have nasty emotional falls too. They may be bleeding and bruised, and deserve to be ministered to with gentleness and compassion also. Men counselors should be as gentle as female counselors.

4. DO WAIT UNTIL A PERSON ASKS FOR PRAYER

Some people want a "ministry" so badly that they are constantly hunting for someone to pray for. They have "itchy fingers." Unless you have a Word from the Lord to go and pray for a particular person, do not do so.

A person may be too courteous and genteel to tell you that they don't want your prayers. If the Holy Spirit has not dug up the ground in their heart, prepared the way, you are out of season with your ministry and the seed may not come to harvest.

5. DO ACCEPT THE PERSON FOR WHOM YOU'RE PRAYING

Unconditional love! And yes, it may be a case of loving the unlovely. We are to hate homosexuality, but accept the person we are praying for as God's child. Hate the sin; love the sinner.

The first time I prayed for a homosexual who had AIDS, I was surprised at my attitude. I thought I would feel . . . "Serves you right for living a promiscuous life-style!" But as that young man stood before me in the prayer line and announced that he was dying of AIDS, my heart broke for him. I looked over his shoulder at his father who was weeping openly, tears running down his cheeks.

I thought, "Oh, my young friend, Jesus Christ died on the cross for you, too. He did not want you to get entangled in a perverted life-style. But He loves you and wants to forgive you."

Don't ever be shocked, repulsed, offended, or angry at anything you hear. There is no room for a pious, "holier-than-thou" attitude in the ministry of inner healing. Nor do you have to have experienced all the sin, perversion, or tragedy in your life in order to minister to people.

I lived in the most loving and protective home ever. The town in which I grew up was very small. (Not one "beer joint" or "dance hall," as the Texas old-timers would say.) I was very naive as I went off to a Baptist university, where I met Ed, my future husband. He grew up in a deeply Christian home also. We were married in a Baptist church, and we attended Baptist services every time the church doors were open. We tithed, read our Bible daily, visited the sick, and both held many church jobs. Our three children were born in a Baptist hospital and later Ed was Academic Vice President of Houston Baptist University. We were "squeaky clean," so to speak, and I praise God for our sheltered lives.

However, when God led me into the ministry of inner healing twenty years later, I heard things (situations, experiences, sins, perversions) confessed to me that I had never heard of and didn't even know existed. In fact, years ago in my early ministry, the first time a transvestite came for prayer, I thought, "What does all this involve, anyway?"

Nevertheless, we as counselors must accept the people just the way they are — warts and all — and love them with Jesus' unconditional love!

We must remember that those in perverted lifestyles usually have deep feelings of shame and guilt. They desperately need prayer to be set free and healed. They come to the WATER to receive a conversion experience with Jesus and His comfort and consolation. They did not come to receive our condemnation and contempt.

6. DO BE PATIENT, PATIENT, PATIENT

In some rare cases, the person you're trying to help will put up a roadblock to ministry (of course, we know where that is coming from — the enemy). They may say something to try to get you angry, or put you off-guard. Don't let them throw you. Some may want to go into every minute, inconsequential detail. Just explain to the person, "We only need a 'thumbnail' sketch — please continue."

However, we cannot let our body language cry out, "Hurry up, you're boring me; I have more important things to do; I'm not interested in you."

We must reach that fine point of balance of allowing the people to share just enough of their deep wounds to enable them to experience a release in their spirit. But also just enough information so that you will know what to pray for in order that they will be healed: spirit, soul, and body.

You may from time to time encounter the following situation: A person will arrive, not wanting to be there AT ALL. They probably were pushed there by a manipulative mother, a nagging wife, or a domineering husband.

A teenager may come in, slouch down in the chair, and glare at you with, "I dare you to help me. You just try!" This is where the patience of the Lord and unconditional love come in. But it's worth it all as the teenager is set free and gives you a great big hug as he or she leaves to go on their way — rejoicing.

7. DO RELY ON THE HOLY SPIRIT

We must always rely on Words of Knowledge and Discernment. We listen to what the people share, but we primarily listen to the Holy Spirit.

We must never fake a Word of Knowledge. We must never make up a personal prophecy just because it sounds good and would be well received by the person. As a person asks, "Do you have a prophecy for me?" (and you don't), just simply and honestly say, "No, I'm sorry, God has not given me a word for you."

We absolutely must rely on the Holy Spirit.

If you deliberately make up some words or call out some spirit because your mind has gone blank and you can't think of anything to say, that is faking it — and it's wrong! Don't fake it! That's deception!

— The person you are praying with knows that you're off base;

— God knows that He didn't give you that word;

— And you certainly know that you're not hearing from the Lord!

There may be times when we are ministering and we call out an unclean spirit or share an insight that the Lord has given us. The person may sit there, look you right in the eye and say, "I don't know what you are talking about." If you prayed before the counseling session, if you prepared your own heart, then trust the leading of the Holy Spirit. However, there are times we, as counselors, may miss it. Whichever the case, don't dwell on it; just continue with the ministering.

Recently, I was back in another state. A girl came up to say, "Mrs. Tapscott, the last time you were here I asked for prayer. You asked me what traumatic thing happened when I was 14. I said nothing did! I lied to you. I was raped when I was 14. I know the Holy Spirit told you that and now I'm ready for you to pray for me again to receive the healing God has for me." Glory to God!

Once in a group meeting I was singled out by the minister, who started praying for me without my asking her. For several minutes she talked about what a sad and tragic childhood I had. She was wrong, ALL WRONG! Nothing could have been farther from the truth. I had a very loving child-hood with loving, Christian parents.

Perhaps I should have stopped her right there or explained to her later that if there was an excess in my family, it was of too much love and that I was showered with love and protection by Christian parents.

In talking to her later, her only comment was, "Well, maybe I was picking up the person next to you." An experience like that can be devastating to a new Christian. It was disturbing to me — a minister. So we must be certain that we are hearing the Holy Spirit. We must never do anything that would embarrass or hurt.

8. DO USE GOOD MANNERS AND BE SENSITIVE

How would you like to be ministered to? With dignity, courtesy, unconditional love, and PLAIN, "old fashion" good manners.

We must remember the tiny, but important, matter of breath mints. If every time you open your mouth your breath odor is unpleasant and literally knocks the person over, it will be hard for them to receive from the Holy Spirit.

Also, if the person to whom you're ministering has been crying so hard that his nose is running and dripping, he may be uncomfortable and self-conscious until he has a tissue to blow his nose. We must be thoughtful, gracious, sensitive, and courteous counselors.

9. DO GIVE ALL THE GORY DETAILS TO THE LORD AFTER MINISTRY

You CAN, and you MUST do this for yourself after each counseling session. Don't allow any sordid, gory details to remain in your mind. I pray for God's protection before each prayer session, not only for myself but also for those in the office. Then, after each session I pray, "God, please cleanse my spirit and soul from anything not of You." I especially rebuke any occult spirits. Ask the Lord to remove any words or pictures in your mind not of Him.

You MUST give all the gory details to the Lord to keep your own mind from being cluttered. Don't let the person share explicit sexual details; that only glorifies Satan.

You MUST give all the grief, sadness, and tragedy up to the Lord so your own spirit will not be weakened or your own heart filled with heaviness and sorrow. You would not be able to continue ministering day in and day out unless you practiced doing this faithfully and "giving this all to Jesus, daily." With all the tragic episodes that you will hear about, you literally cannot take them on yourself. They might open a door allowing depression or other spirits to enter you. You MUST give them to the Lord. From time to time you will need someone to pray for you, just in case you have picked up some oppression, etc.

In fact . . .

A prayer counselor ministering inner healing regularly needs as much personal inner healing as possible.

---

10.   DO LIFT UP THE NAME OF JESUS

In the entire experience of inner healing, the most important thing of all is to *lift up the name of Jesus and to give Him all the praise and glory.* Praise Him for each transformed life, each healed memory, each bondage broken. Our utmost concern as a minister of inner healing should be to make certain that everything we say or do is based on the inspired Word of God — the Bible.

CHAPTER NINE

MINISTERING DON'TS

". . . Correct and rebuke your people when they need it, encourage them to do right, and all the time be feeding them patiently with God's Word" (2 Timothy 4:2b, TLB).

1. DON'T HEAP GUILT OR CONDEMNATION

We must never judge or rate sin. We don't know how God looks at the different sins. Our own self-righteousness and spiritual pride might be just as offensive to God as someone else's adultery, addiction, or abortion.

We cannot — we must not — minister with harsh legalism, hitting the person again and again with Bible verses. The sword of the Spirit is to set people free from bondage, not to kill the "walking wounded." A minister who had a photographic memory said that he could literally "kill" someone with the Bible if he wanted to. He could prove anything with a verse, and use it as a sword to pierce the already shattered and bleeding heart of the counselee. We must love and not condemn the people for whom we pray.

We must also have forgiveness in our own hearts for those people who have sinned against society and the Body of Christ.

The minister from up east who committed adultery and had to leave his church also needs our forgiveness. Perhaps if his church had been praying harder for him and his family, this tragedy might not have occurred.

When the leaders of a Christian organization sin against society and the entire Body of Christ, we are all wounded by their actions! Nevertheless, we must forgive them and pray God's blessings on them.

In each case we should say, ''There but for the grace of God could go each one of us.'' Lord, let us each one show Your mercy. The Bible says, *''For there will be no mercy to those who have shown no mercy. But if you have been merciful, then God's mercy toward you will win out over his judgment against you''* (James 2:13, TLB).

WE MUST NEVER COMPROMISE OUR BELIEFS, BUT WE MUST ALWAYS SHOW THE LOVING, COMPASSIONATE, FORGIVING SIDE OF JESUS.

"We must not judge, lest we be judged" (see Matthew 7:1; Luke 6:37, KJV).

When a leader falls, it is usually because no Aaron and Hur were there to hold up his arms like they did for Moses. *"As long as Moses held up his hands, the Israelites were winning, but whenever he lowered his hands, the Amalekites were winning. When Moses' hands grew tired, they took a stone and put it under him and he sat on it. Aaron and Hur held his hands up — one on one side, one on the other — so that his hands remained steady . . ."* (Exodus 17:11-12, NIV).

2. DON'T BREAK CONFIDENCES

Don't share with your mate, children, best friend, or your prayer group who came to you for prayer, or what the problems were about. I always pray that the Lord will take from my mind the memories of the people that I pray with. I know that God does this because many times someone has mentioned my praying for them, and I do not remember it at all.

We as counselors should be "priest-like" in adhering to the sacred secrecy of confession. God has called me to minister to and pray inner healing for pastors and their wives. They, of all people, must have the complete assurance that absolutely nothing will ever be shared.

3. DON'T "LET ON" PUBLICLY THAT YOU'VE PRAYED FOR SOMEONE

Usually a person absolutely does not want anyone to know that he or she came for prayer. When you say in public, "How are you? Are you feeling better?" And if these and other questions are asked with a "knowing look" then these comments are a giveaway that you have prayed inner healing for them. We need to watch our words, as well as our actions. We need to be very sensitive to another's need for privacy, especially those who are in leadership.

4. DON'T SHOUT LOUDLY

It's not how loudly we shout — it is the power of Jesus and His anointing that breaks the yoke, that sets free, that heals and transforms. God hears the tiniest whisper — the tiniest.

At the time I was writing this book, I received a call from a minister in another city. He related that in a church meeting he had asked for a visiting evangelist to pray for his hearing because he was going deaf. The evangelist had shouted very loudly in his ear as he bound the spirit of deafness. The man's eardrum was permanently damaged (he believes) from the incredibly loud shout, and now his hearing is almost gone.

God is not deaf. He hears our prayers. We need to pray with confidence, boldness, and authority yes, but not in an extremely loud voice. Praying loudly in a group brings attention to the person praying, not to the ministry of Jesus. Again, let me emphasize, we don't have to scream, shout, pound the person, "carry on" or put on a show. It is the anointing of Jesus that breaks the yoke, not our loud voices or antics.

REMEMBER —

Just because a person is domineering and loud does not mean he has more power or anointing. Gentleness and quietness are certainly not signs of weakness, nor the lack of power and anointing from the Lord.

---

5. DON'T PUT HANDS ALL OVER PEOPLE

To some people, having hands laid all over them is very annoying and disturbing.

In fact, I can remember an episode of being prayed for by a very loud and zealous group of ladies when I was a new babe in the Spirit. I did not like their hands on my neck, head, shoulders, and arms. I did not like having a dozen ladies praying loudly in the Spirit for me (right in my ears) all at once. It was frightening and offensive at the time.

Today it would not bother me, but we must remember that we may also be praying for another brand-new Christian, or someone newly baptized in the Spirit. These actions may be very foreign and offensive to them, also.

I recall another episode when Ed and I spoke one morning at a church. There was a new couple visiting the church that Sunday. Not only had they never been to that church, they had never been to ANY Spirit-filled church before.

With that in mind, we were very careful not to offend or frighten them. We prayed for them very quietly and gently. The power of the Lord came over the man and he rested in the Spirit.

We turned to pray for the next person. I glanced back at the visitor on the floor and, to my utter chagrin, another visitor was bending over the man, rubbing his neck and head. We were aghast, and quickly and discreetly asked the person to please allow him to rest in the Spirit undisturbed.

We must remember to be very careful about where we put our hands when praying for people. Hands were made for holding hands or touching shoulders when praying in a counseling situation. Hands were made to lay hands on the sick that they might be made whole, but we must do so in a proper and gentle way.

6. DON'T BE AFRAID TO BE FIRM

There are times that we must be very firm with our instructions and guidance. Firm, yes, but always with Christian love and compassion.

For example:

If the person has been involved in the occult: witchcraft, ESP, EST, fortunetelling, pendulum swinging, automatic writing, astrology, astral projection, or seances, then the person absolutely must throw away all objects, books, calendars, and charts that have anything to do with the occult. This includes anything given to you by a curandero or by the imposter who makes a person think that they can communicate with the dead through seances.

As the prayer counselor, we must have the counselee renounce the occult, ask forgiveness from God, and throw away everything involved with the occult practice, and completely turn their back on this demonic activity. If they do not do this, they will not be set free.

Example two:

When a homosexual or lesbian comes for prayer counseling and deliverance we have to ask some questions. "Do you truly want to be free? Do you really want to turn your back on this perverted life-style?"

If they are sincere, then we must go one step more. We must tell them that, in order to be free, they will have to leave the homosexual community and the homosexual "friend" with whom they have been living. It is imperative to get away from that environment of perversion.

A young man who had been disguising himself as a woman and was a pianist with a band came for a "last minute" prayer before he had a sex change to become a woman. I think he must have come only to appease his frantic parents.

Ed and I prayed and counseled him all one Saturday afternoon. The glory and power of the Lord filled the room. The young man repented. He prayed, asking God to deliver and set him free from his perverted life-style. He recommitted his life to the Lord and received his prayer language. It was truly a glorious and beautiful time with the Lord.

The young man's countenance was clean and he had a glow about him. He said, "I'm going to cancel the surgery." He explained that it was very difficult to be approved for this type of surgery because you had to be approved by a doctor, a psychiatrist, and a minister. But he said, "I'm free at last and I'm going to cancel the surgery."

He had left all his belongings — musical equipment (dresses), etc., in another state. We encouraged him to just have his musical instruments mailed to him and please NOT go back into that pit of deception. We told him that Satan would try to ensnare him again.

For three months he was involved in church fellowship — living, walking, and talking a Spirit-filled life. His family was thrilled.

Then he decided he was strong enough to go get all of his belongings; but when he returned to that den of iniquity (of drugs, alcohol, rock music and sexual perversion), the temptation was too strong and he went back to living the lie that he was a girl.

His heartbroken mother wrote us the news — her son had the sex change operation after all. He was now a girl. The experience was so devastating to the family that the father died from a heart attack immediately following the son's surgery.

The mother wrote, thanking us for praying with her son and also praising God for the time that her son had walked with the Lord. During that time, she wrote, he was the son that she knew God gave her and meant for him to be. She thanked us for trying to help him. She said, "I know he could have remained free if he hadn't gone back around that life-style again."

So — this is the reason why we as counselors must be firm even if they don't always listen!

7. DON'T EVER, EVER, EVER SAY "IF YOU HAD MORE FAITH, YOU WOULD BE HEALED"

So many times I have heard Fr. Bob DeGrandis warn his audiences about not making this offensive statement to the person they are praying with. We offend, threaten, and put a load of guilt on people by saying this. It is not the amount of faith that heals! It is God's grace and mercy and by His Spirit.

Consider the little child, or a person in a coma — can they exemplify faith? No! But many times they are healed! There have been other times when "saints" of God have had faith to move mountains and yet for some reason they did not receive their healing. Then I have seen God heal people who had absolutely no faith whatsoever. Some were not even Christians. Just read the next story.

In 1985 in Dusseldorf, Germany, a young man dressed in punk rock fashion came to a meeting at the Jesus House. He had on black leather pants, coat, shoes, and shirt. He had on lots of silver jewelry and studs on his clothes. His hair stood straight up about four inches in the air.

I called out a Word of Knowledge of the Lord healing someone's wrist. It was the punk rocker's wrist that was healed. Then the Lord revealed that He had healed someone's shoulder. It was this same young man — the punk rocker. Praise the Lord!

When I asked him to come to the platform, you can imagine my surprise when I found out that he was not a Christian. That bit of news blew my theology right there. But, praise the Lord, the young man accepted Jesus and was baptized in the Holy Spirit.

Harold* then asked if he could bring his wife to the next meeting, and we said, "Of course." He hesitantly and sheepishly added, "Well, she's really not my wife. We're just living together." He took a deep breath, paused and added, "And she's pregnant."

I encouraged him, "Please bring her. I want to meet her." (And I truly did.) "She needs to find the Lord and also be baptized in the Holy Spirit."

So "Ms. Punk Rocker" came to the next meeting. She was also dressed all in black. Mr. and Ms. Punk Rocker sat center, front row, and the good news, the glorious good news — she accepted the Lord and was baptized in the Holy Spirit. One of my most precious memories was forming a circle with this couple and having them lift me up in prayer before I left. I encouraged them to make their marriage legal, to get involved in a church, and to turn their backs on the world of drugs.

This experience really showed me something. It's not the amount of faith we have that heals. It

---

*Name has been changed.

is not our Christianity. It is not the person's faith, but it is God's grace and mercy that heals.

8. DON'T GO LOOKING FOR DEMONS

We must never become so out-of-balance that we are always demon hunting. Looking for "demons behind every door," and "spirits behind every sneeze."

We should not be afraid of demons, nor be overly interested in them. I firmly believe it is unwise to seek to have the demon speak to you, to ask his name, or how many there are, etc. Satan is the master deceiver — how can we believe him? We need to use the discernment that God gives us and when there is an evil spirit present, then quietly but with the POWER, AUTHORITY, and ANOINTING of Jesus Christ, cast it out. A person being set free (the experience of deliverance) is like a butterfly coming forth gently from a cocoon, being changed into a new creature. A gloriously transformed person is a beautiful miracle of God.

9. DON'T GIVE A LOT OF ADVICE

You are hearing only one side of the story of a troubled marriage. One must never *EVER* advise divorce — unless you are absolutely certain of all the circumstances. We must be prudent with giving advice.

For example, a young mother from another city discovered that her husband had been sexually abusing their three-year-old daughter. She had separated from her husband, but was counseled by her pastor to return to the marriage and "stand" for his deliverance and healing of their marriage. She went back to her husband — against her better judgment and motherly instincts. The father again molested the child.

Fortunately, an Aglow officer recommended that the mother take the child and leave her husband immediately — which she did. The Aglow officer also suggested that she come to me for inner healing.

I was horrified when I heard this story. I ministered to both the mother and daughter, and I was inclined to agree with the Aglow officer that divorce seemed to be the only alternative to protect the child. In fact, I felt that God would hold the mother responsible for staying in a relationship (I don't call this a marriage in any sense of the word) that subjected her baby to this horrible sexual abuse.

The child was suffering from a vaginal infection as well as kidney and bladder infections. Can you imagine the fear, emotional trauma, and pain of that child? After much, much prayer, mother and daughter both were gradually healed of this horrendous experience.

———————

Another woman was married to a sadist. He frequently tried to kill her. She had awakened several times during the night when he was trying to strangle her, or smother her with a pillow. Frequently he held guns on the entire family telling them he was going to shoot them all. She had bruises on her body almost constantly from his severe beatings — black eyes, a broken nose, swollen, lacerated cheeks. She said that she stopped counting the broken ribs where he had kicked her. Why was she staying in such a life-threatening relationship? Because she was so battered and abused and sick herself that she was afraid to leave. Her will was broken. Her sons' lives were destroyed on alcohol and drugs. One son was in prison.

After much prayer and deliberation, I advised her that she should leave or divorce her husband.[1] Much to my relief, she said, "Well, that's confirmation because my pastor and a Christian psychologist said the very same thing." Praise the Lord Jesus.

———————

A schoolteacher brought her fiance to Ed and me for prayer and for advice about getting married. I immediately felt there was a deceiving spirit in the man, even something very evil. As firmly as possible (after the counseling session was over), I recommended that they not get married. The man was furious at me, which only added to my suspicions about him.

———

[1]We must be aware that as counselors we might be held legally responsible for any guidance given. Use much wisdom. Always remember that we have life and death in our mouths. We will be held responsible for what we say — not only to God but perhaps to man. We must listen to the Holy Spirit and only say what He tells us.

Sadly to say, they did not take our advice, or that of others, and married. In a very short time, the lady discovered that she had married a deceiving and very emotionally sick man, in fact, a psychopath. He threatened her life several times in just a few weeks time. She quickly divorced him, but was left with deep, emotional scars. Praise God that since that horrible experience, God has healed and she is happily married to a Spirit-filled Christian.

We must *never, never* recommend separation or divorce unless we are absolutely (without a shadow of a doubt) certain it is for the safety of the client, and that everything has been done that can be done to save the marriage.

10. DON'T GIVE PERSONAL PROPHECY UNLESS YOU KNOW IT'S OF THE LORD

Praise God for true prophets of God. I know several personally and have been ministered to by the Lord through them.

However (and unfortunately), there are those who want to have the Gift of Prophecy but don't! They are making up nice-sounding little phrases that are not coming from the Lord. This is a form of deception. Prophecy must come directly from the Lord, with the power of a two-edged sword (see Hebrews 4:12, KJV) and His anointing.

There are times when a false, personal prophecy is given and the person receiving it does exactly what the person giving the prophecy said to do — with disastrous results, because it was not from the Lord.

A pastor's wife in another state shared how a couple had been prophesying to young couples to "Sell your possessions, quit your jobs, and live by faith." She sadly said that she personally knew of two couples who had followed these false prophecies and were now living out of their cars, disillusioned with God and "His" gifts.

A girl came for prayer for inner healing after a disastrous experience. A visiting evangelist had given a prophecy that she was to marry a certain man in her church. Two other people, one man and one woman in her church, also "confirmed" the prophecy. The girl, to her dismay and heartache, found out AFTER the marriage ceremony that the man was still married to another woman, and in fact, was a "con artist."

We must be so certain that the prophecy we give is of the Lord — God will hold us responsible for every word we utter. (I must add that He will also hold us responsible if we do not give the message He tells us to give. And we will miss God's blessing by being disobedient.)

The Bible says, *"Dearly Loved Friends, don't always believe everything you hear just because someone says it is a message from God: test it first to see if it really is . . ."* (1 John 4:1, TLB).

CHAPTER TEN

THE COUNSELING SESSION

". . . A son is given to us! . . . He will be called 'Wonderful Counselor . . .'" (Isaiah 9:6, St. Jerome).

"Yes, it was God who sent me here . . . and he has made me a counselor . . ." (Genesis 45:8, TLB).

Before a person comes for prayer counseling, I usually ask that they read my book on inner healing, or at least my pamphlet on inner healing.[1] They need to know exactly what to expect during the counseling session.

If parents are calling to make an appointment for their teenager, I make certain that the teenager is agreeable to coming. If a child does not want to come and feels coerced into coming, then they may

---

[1]*Inner Healing Through Healing of Memories* and inner healing pamphlets by Betty Tapscott may be ordered from Tapscott Ministries, P.O. Box 19827, Houston, Texas 77224 (1-713-558-3703).

sit with arms folded, mind closed, and be very belligerent the entire time of the counseling session. It is a waste of time for both of you, and all who are involved.

———————

The following guidelines explain in a very simple way the steps I usually use in praying for inner healing.

As we begin the prayer counseling session, I always have an opening prayer something like this:

Dear Lord, thank You for this person who is before me. Lord, You knew about this time of sharing since before time began. Thank You, Father, for Your Holy Spirit. Thank You for stationing Your ministering angels all about. Thank You for Your love, protection, and guidance.

Lord, we commit this time to You — every thought and every word. Jesus, speak through me today.

Father, in the name of Jesus I ask that You would free (use their name) today from any fear or nervousness. I pray that this person will be set free and that all bondage will be broken. I pray that, as a butterfly in a cocoon, he or she will come forth into a shining new life.

Dear Lord, give (use name) a tranquil mind, because Your Word says, "A tranquil mind gives life to the flesh" (Psalm 14:30, RSV).

The Counseling Session

*Lord, we are thanking You in advance for what You
are going to do today. All praise and glory go to You. In
Jesus' name. Amen.*

HOW LONG IS THE SESSION?

There was a time that I allowed three to four
hours for a session. Logistically, a counselor cannot
spend this much time. I now allow forty-five minutes
to one hour for the person to share. Then I spend the
rest of the time in prayer and counseling.[2]

During the session, don't interrupt as the person
is speaking — except to direct your questions, and
to keep the session moving smoothly and not off on
a tangent.

EXPLAIN THE PLAN OF SALVATION

In the beginning moments of the session I ask
the question, "When did you invite Jesus into your
heart?" or "Tell me about your conversion experience." You would be surprised at the number
of people who have doubts about their salvation.
Salvation is the most important healing of all; it is
our foundation. It is the meaning of our life here on

---

[2]I've had to limit my counseling because I spend most of my time
out of the office holding seminars on inner healing, teaching others how
to minister inner healing. The Lord has told me, however, to pray with
pastors and their wives, or those emergency cases that He sends.

111

earth. A right relationship with Jesus is our only hope for lasting joy, love, and peace. Salvation is our only way to eternal life — Heaven.

"For God loved the world so much that he gave his only son so that anyone who believes in him shall not perish but have eternal life" (John 3:16, TLB).

I usually have every person pray a prayer of commitment to Jesus — before we pray for inner healing.

Prayer for Salvation

Lord Jesus, I know I am a sinner and have sinned. I confess my sins to You. I ask forgiveness of all my sins — those I remember and those sins I've forgotten about. I forgive those who have sinned against me.

Lord Jesus, come into my heart as my Saviour. I surrender my life to You. I make You Lord of my heart and life. I commit myself totally and completely to You. Thank You for coming into my heart as my personal Saviour. I love You, Jesus, and want to serve You forever. Amen.

DISCUSS FORGIVENESS

I explain to the people that forgiveness is the key to emotional healing, and that they must forgive:

Others

Themselves

God

God is sovereign and does no wrong, but many times a person is angry and blames God. The person needs to be reminded also, that:

**FORGIVENESS IS NOT A FEELING
BUT AN ACT OF THE WILL.**

If they say, "I can't forgive," don't make them feel guilty. Simply say, "Why don't you ask Jesus to forgive the person through you?" Tell them they should repeat each day, "Lord, I forgive (name the person). Lord, I forgive (name the person)." Finally, they will be able to say, "Lord, bless (name the person)." I always share that I know it is easy for a counselor to say, "forgive," but that I'm sure it is another thing to have to walk in their shoes.

EXPLAIN THE TWO STEPS OF INNER HEALING

Step 1: Explain the Breaking of Bondages

The counselee may be a little nervous about what all will take place. Tell them that first you will ask the Lord to break any chains keeping them in bondage. Share the following Scriptures with the person, and others listed in chapter two.

"For God will break the chains that bind his people and the whip that scourges them . . ." (Isaiah 9:4, TLB).

"Whatever you bind on earth is bound in heaven and whatever you free on earth is freed in heaven" (Matthew 18:18, TLB).

I seldom use the term "deliverance" or "demons." I find that this tends to frighten children or make adults wonder if they are demon-possessed. Tell the client that the emotional wounds must be cleansed (of any unforgiveness, hate, bitterness, etc.), before they will be healed. I explain that we will ask the Lord to break the bondage of rejection, fear, insecurity, unworthiness, etc.

I often use the term "killing giants." A client will understand the term ("Giant of Depression") and not be frightened. I always assure them that Christians cannot be POSSESSED, only OPPRESSED.

Step 2: Explain the Healing of Memories

After the prayer for breaking bondages, I explain the manner in which we pray for healing of memories; and that it is simply asking Jesus to heal hurts. The Word says, *"Jesus Christ is the same yesterday, today and forever"* (Hebrews 13:8, TLB). That means He knew about us before we were born. He knows about all the painful memories. Explain to them that we pray for each year of their life. (One of the reasons to do this is in order that the counselee will not become anxious about the length of time spent in prayer.)

I also assure them that the Holy Spirit will not embarrass them in any way. This may alleviate some dread or nervousness. We must pray with sincerity, gentleness, compassion, and under the anointing of the Holy Spirit.

BEFORE THE PRAYER

Before starting the prayer on inner healing, I always ask the person some very simple and practical questions (don't laugh, it's important).

— Do you need to go to the bathroom?

— Do you need a drink of water?

— Do you want to sit or kneel while praying?

I know some counselors who have the counselee lie down on a couch. I find this unacceptable. Sitting on a comfortable chair or sofa is much more non-threatening to a counselee. Some counselees do prefer to kneel, especially your liturgical Christians.

Many times I have held the very young children in my arms. I have even sat down on the floor with them to pray. The question should be: where would the person be more comfortable and at ease? Where would they be more open to the Holy Spirit?

MINISTERING INNER HEALING

We must have guidelines, but we must never be so regimented that we won't follow the leading of the Holy Spirit. Above all, we must listen to His guidance and be obedient in the manner of ministering.

As I have mentioned before, the way God taught me to pray for inner healing is in this order:

— Prayer for binding and casting out the various unclean spirits.

— Prayer for healing of memories.

But these steps should only be used as guidelines. We cannot box God in. And we can always *expect the unexpected.*

Occasionally God has me pray for the healing of memories first, then pray for the bondages to be broken. You will find that at times God will intermingle the two steps all through the prayer.

The forgiveness prayer can be at the beginning, at the end, or as each episode and traumatic experience surfaces during the time of healing of memories.

The thing to remember is that FORGIVENESS is the key to their healing. We must take time to have them verbalize each statement of forgiveness for each person who has hurt them.

It is important to pray that God will fill the person with love, joy, peace, and all the fruit of the Spirit, plus pray that they will be filled to overflowing with the Holy Spirit after the prayer for inner healing.

EXPLAIN THE BAPTISM IN THE HOLY SPIRIT

After the inner healing prayer, I always explain the baptism in the Holy Spirit. I point out the related Scripture verses in Acts and Corinthians. Usually they are receptive to receiving the infilling of the Holy Spirit.

When they realize that praying in the Spirit is the last part of the armor of God, they quickly say, "I need all that God has for me. Please pray that I will be filled to overflowing with the Holy Spirit and receive my prayer language." I always share that we should seek the "giver" and not the "gift," and that praying in the Spirit does not make us any better than anyone else — just better than we were.

ANOINT WITH OIL

James 5:14, TLB, says, *"Is anyone sick? He should call for the elders of the church and they should pray over him and pour a little oil upon him, calling on the Lord to heal him, for the Lord will make him well; and if his sickness was caused by some sin, the Lord will forgive him."*

117

I firmly believe this Scripture means emotional healing, as well. So I always anoint with oil, asking that the Lord heal: spirit, soul, and body. Usually the person, when they are anointed and have the "laying on of hands," will rest in the Spirit. Frequently they receive physical healing while the Lord is blessing them this way. (Not only physical healing, but emotional and spiritual healing as well.)

WARN THEM OF SPIRITUAL WARFARE

Sometimes a person will come for counseling, receive healing of memories, and think, "Well, praise God! I'm healed! — and that's that!" The person needs to know that he or she may be in for a rough spiritual battle. Satan will be furious that they asked for forgiveness, have forgiven, and were set free and healed.

Explain the basic facts of spiritual warfare.

"Be careful — watch out for attacks from Satan, your great enemy. He prowls around like a hungry, roaring lion, looking for some victim to tear apart. Stand firm when he attacks. Trust the Lord . . ." (1 Peter 5:8-9, TLB).

". . . I can do everything God asks me to with the help of Christ who gives me the strength and power" (Philippians 4:13, TLB).

"Where the Spirit of the Lord is, there is liberty" (2 Corinthians 3:17, KJV).

". . . if the Son sets you free, you will indeed be free . . ." (John 8:36, TLB).

Remind the person that they are not to keep their eyes on Satan, but on Jesus. However, they need to be equipped and prepared to fight the enemy without fear.

REASSURE YOUR COUNSELEE

As they are leaving, they need to be assured and reminded of several things:

— That what they have shared with you is a sacred trust and that it will not be revealed to anyone. (We must keep that vow.)

— Remind them one more time that inner healing is a process, not a one-time experience.

— I usually explain that they may feel as if they have had surgery — in fact, they did — surgery of the soul. After any physical surgery, there needs to be a time of recovery. It may take time to get over spiritual surgery, also.

— Some people may feel a little tired, shaky, weak; others feel absolutely great. I usually encourage a person, if at all possible, to go home, rest, listen to Christian music, and meditate before the Lord. I advise them to allow the Lord to continue to minister to them after the prayer for inner healing.

— Most of the people after prayer for inner healing feel great, just absolutely wonderful. They feel as if a weight has been lifted from their chest, and that all oppression is gone. They are filled with a peace and joy that they have never had before. Usually, their face is glowing with the love of Jesus. They are transformed and leave praising the Lord.

— One of the last things that I share with a client is *how to keep their inner healing.* Because of the importance of those guidelines, we are putting them into a separate chapter.

— Remind them that — GOD DID HIS PART; AS A COUNSELOR, YOU DID YOURS; AND THAT THEY WILL HAVE TO DO THEIR PART TO KEEP THEIR INNER HEALING.

— As they go out the door, I often tell them of God's love letter to them: *"You are precious to me and honored and I love you"* (Isaiah 43:4, TLB).

CHAPTER ELEVEN

HOW TO KEEP
YOUR INNER HEALING[1]

*"O Lord, you have freed me from my bonds.
And I will serve you forever. I will worship you
and offer you a sacrifice of thanksgiving"*
(Psalm 116:16, TLB).

Suppose you have been prayed for, and the Lord
has done a tremendous and beautiful inner healing.
You feel like a different person; every fiber of your
being is filled with peace, joy, and love. You are
completely set free from any bondage, and all painful memories are totally healed . . . but . . . if you
invite those negative attitudes and confessions
back, if you deliberately start dwelling on the old
wounds, they will certainly give you trouble again.

Think of it this way: Haven't you seen a child
with a skinned knee? It is healing beautifully — but
then he starts rubbing and scratching the scab, and

[1]Taken from *Inner Healing Through Healing of Memories* © 1975
by Betty Tapscott. Also in pamphlet form © 1973. May be ordered
from P.O. Box 19827, Houston, TX 77224.

before long the wound is an open sore again. We must forget the past and look to the future. We must not reopen healing wounds.

I want to share some things with you that will help you keep your inner or physical healing.

1. PRAY WITHOUT CEASING

Live in an attitude of prayer. Wake up with a prayer and go to sleep with a prayer on your lips. Pray about all things . . . big or small. Pray when you are driving the car, before you answer the phone, as you're shopping, etc. *"Pray without ceasing"* (1 Thessalonians 5:17, KJV).

2. READ YOUR BIBLE REGULARLY

Just as you must have physical food to survive physically, you must have spiritual food to survive spiritually. You get that spiritual food from reading God's Word. Read your Bible every day.

3. PRAISE THE LORD ALWAYS

Develop a positive outlook. In 1 Thessalonians 5:16-18, TLB, the Bible says, *"Always be joyful. Always keep on praying. No matter what happens, always be thankful, for this is God's will for you who belong to Christ Jesus."* So praise God in all circumstances. Do not give way to negative confessions. Praise God for your hurts, praise Him for your painful memories, and praise Him for your problems! *"Always give thanks for everything . . ."* (Ephesians 5:20, TLB).

4. DAILY COMMIT YOURSELF TO THE LORD

Daily ask for His guidance and wisdom. Give up all practices that do not glorify the Lord. Ask the Holy Spirit to reveal to you the things you are doing that are not pleasing to the Lord, and then . . . stop doing them! Don't say you can't stop some habit. The Bible says that we can do all things through Christ who strengthens us (see Philippians 4:13, KJV). Each morning say, "Lord, I commit this day to You — every thought, word, and deed." Pray daily to be filled with the fruit of the Spirit: love, joy, peace, patience, kindness, goodness, faithfulness, gentleness, and self-control (Galatians 5:22-23, TLB).

Also, each morning read Ephesians 6:13-18. These verses will tell you how to put on the whole armor of God. Verse 13 tells us to *"Use every piece of God's armor to resist the enemy whenever he attacks, and when it is all over, you will still be standing up"* (Ephesians 6:13, TLB).

5. DEDICATE YOUR HOME TO THE LORD

Surround yourself with spiritual things that glorify the Lord. Listen to Christian music, read Christian books, subscribe to Christian magazines, listen to Spirit-filled tapes. (We never go on a long trip without a tape recorder and cassettes by Spirit-filled musicians and teachers. We listen until we reach our destination.) Throw away all books, magazines, pictures, articles, and music that do not glorify the Lord. Choose television programs carefully, not only for your children but for yourself. Ask yourself, "If Jesus walked into this room, would I have this particular show on?" Also, be very careful which movies you allow your children to see or the ones you see.

I realize there must be a balance in our lives. Someone has said we can become so "heavenly minded" we are no "earthly" good. I'm just saying we must put the Lord first in every area of our lives. Pray for a perfect balance of being in the world but not of the world. Jesus does not honor compromise.

6. STAND FIRM AGAINST SATAN

Take authority over Satan when he comes against you, and bind him in the name of Jesus (see Matthew 12:29, TLB). If a spirit of fear is bothering you, say, "You spirit of fear, I cast you out in the name of Jesus" (see Mark 16:17, TLB). Remember,

". . . Resist the devil and he will flee from you" (James 4:7, TLB). Keep repeating over and over, *"perfect love casts out all fear"* (see 1 John 4:18, KJV). We need to keep our eyes on Jesus and not on Satan. But God warns us to *"Be careful — watch out for attacks from Satan, your great enemy. He prowls around like a hungry, roaring lion, looking for some victim to tear apart. Stand firm when he attacks"* (1 Peter 5:8-9, TLB).

7. GET INTO A SPIRIT-FILLED FELLOWSHIP

If your church does not teach that Jesus Christ died for your sins, find a church that does. Ask the Holy Spirit to lead you to a prayer group where you can sense the power of the Holy Spirit and the moving of the Holy Spirit. Make the effort to go hear Christian speakers and take your family with you.

8. HAVE A PRAYER PARTNER

You need a prayer partner, one with whom you can share your burdens and praises. The Bible says, *". . . if two of you agree down here on earth concerning anything you ask for, my Father in heaven will do it for you"* (Matthew 18:19, TLB). If you feel Satan coming against you, and if after you pray, the oppression still doesn't leave, then ask your prayer partner to pray with you immediately. Remember, prayer partners — "Do not share these requests with anyone else but the Lord!"

9. ACCEPT GOD'S INNER HEALING

Accept the inner healing that God gives you. Accept it by faith. You may say, "I don't have enough faith." The Bible says we only need to have faith as big as a grain of mustard seed (see Matthew 17:20). If you don't have even that much faith, then have faith in the faith of Jesus. Don't look at the evidence or the circumstances but stand on God's promises. The Bible says life or death is in your mouth. Only let positive confessions come from your mouth.

10. CONSTANTLY FORGIVE AND RESTORE

The moment someone hurts you, give it to the Lord immediately. Not that night, not the next day, but right then. The moment you hurt someone, say, "I'm sorry, forgive me," and ask God's forgiveness. Go into the "construction" business, constructing bridges between broken relationships. If you have offended someone openly, ask their forgiveness. But if they are not aware of your inner feelings, be silent. Ask God's forgiveness for your ugly attitude.

Don't go charging up to someone with piety and say, "I've always thought you were terrible, I really couldn't tolerate you, but now I'm sorry, will you forgive me?'' Obviously that would do more harm than good. If you each know there have been harsh words, dishonesty, gossip, or false accusations, go to that person and ask their forgiveness. Don't stop there! If you have spread false rumors, try to repair the damage you have caused. Try to restore and rebuild every broken relationship. Share God's love and His peace continually with others.

11. RECEIVE THE EUCHARIST (COMMUNION, "THE LORD'S SUPPER") REGULARLY

There is HEALING in receiving the Eucharist often. Most Protestants usually receive it once a month. Episcopalians, Catholics, and others fortunately are able to receive it daily. When we have cleansed our hearts, taken Communion in the right attitude, and trusted God expectantly — then many times healing will take place: either spirit, soul, or body.

12. REACH OUT TO OTHERS

Sometimes we are so involved in our own problems, hurts, and woundedness that we don't reach out to others to help them. But if we will say, ''Lord, may I be an instrument of blessing to someone today? May I bring Your peace, love, and joy to someone who is hurting today?" Then, in so doing, we will discover that as we give out, we too shall receive healing ourselves. Praise the Lord!

Retaining your inner healing may not be easy, but remember you are the only one who can keep the inner healing God provided for you. God will do His part, but you have to do your part!

Certainly, you may have valleys, disappointments, and failures. We all do; life is a constant climb up the ladder toward God. We may climb up three rungs of the ladder and slip down one. We may climb up five and slip back four. But WE CAN BE OVERCOMERS by resting in the Lord, by submitting to Him, obeying Him, by leaning on Him, by trusting Him.

Imagine yourself in a boat with Jesus as the captain. The seas may be very rough and treacherous, the wind blowing with a mighty gale, the rain falling in torrents, the lightning striking all around you. But with Jesus as your captain, He will calm that storm, He will guide your ship safely home, He will keep you in the hollow of His hand.

We Can Be Victorious!

We Can Be OVERCOMERS!

CHAPTER TWELVE

WORDS OF CAUTION

"Trust in the LORD with all your heart. Never rely on what you think you know. Remember the LORD in everything you do, and he will show you the right way. Never let yourself think that you are wiser than you are; simply obey the LORD and refuse to do wrong. If you do, it will be like good medicine, healing your wounds and easing your pains" (Proverbs 3:5-8, St. Jerome).

As prayer counselors or ministers of inner healing we must be careful that we don't ever use the Bible as a sword to "kill" rather than to set the captive free. We must minister in love and compassion, and not legalism.

Be alert and watch for any symptoms of transference to the prayer counselor from the counselees. You may become a substitute mother or father, wife or husband to them. They may become so dependent that they cannot make a decision, or fight a spiritual battle without you. They may begin to develop an unhealthy love attachment to you. This has to be broken immediately.

Be very careful about how you hug. What might be a gentle brotherly or sisterly hug to you might be sexually stimulating to someone else.

I have often shared with pastors and their wives that in their congregations they perhaps should encourage the hugging of men with men, and women with women.

I recall a male counselor sitting on the floor at a seminar who was holding a woman, kissing her repeatedly on her forehead, in order, as he explained, to give her the Father's love. To those standing around, it looked completely out of line and inappropriate.

There must be no hint of impropriety. All things must be aboveboard and pure. Ask yourself, "How would this look to a stranger walking by?" It may be perfectly innocent, but does it look that way to an outsider?

Unfortunately, I have seen people counseling or praying at conferences where the man praying has the woman counselee backed up against the wall. The thought passed through my mind, "Is this prayer, or is it a form of seduction? Is the counselor playing a sexual game?'' There is absolutely no place for this type of behavior in ministry.

When praying for men for physical healing, I usually have Joe (my office manager) place his hand on the man's chest, low back, etc. Men counselors — place your hand only on a woman's head, shoulder, or arm (lightly).

Use all precaution and pray with purity and holiness. Remember, the person may feel very vulnerable. Their emotional state may be fragile. Deep feelings are brought to the surface. Everything that is said and done must be strictly professional and completely Christlike.

I've mentioned this before, but it bears saying again. We must never tell a person to stop taking any kind of medicine: heart or blood pressure medication, insulin, or medicine for deep depression, etc. When they are healed by God, their doctor will know it and will rejoice also.

Don't "put down" organizations, such as Alcoholics Anonymous, Weight Watchers, etc. These organizations have their place and have helped thousands of people. However, try to lead your counselees to place themselves in God's hands and not just a source.

Watch for burnout in your own life. Don't overdo, over-commit. Take time for yourself — for rest and times of refreshing. Since burnout is such a prevalent problem, I've included an entire chapter on this subject.

CHAPTER THIRTEEN

HOW TO PREVENT BURNOUT

". . . For you are God's temple, the home of the living God, and God has said of you, 'I will live in them and walk among them, and I will be their God and they shall be my people' " (2 Corinthians 6:16, TLB).

There may not be another type of ministry that requires as much energy as praying for inner healing. You usually cannot check arms and legs to make sure that they are the same length, quickly pray for the back, and presto, the person is healed emotionally. (Although God can do *anything* He wants to, *any way* He wants to.)

In the ministry of inner healing it requires time to find out what the root problem is. The Holy Spirit will reveal it quickly, but we must allow the person time to tear down the wall that he or she has built around themselves.

We must *listen* intently with the ears of Jesus to the person with whom we are ministering inner

133

healing, and that takes time and much energy. Many counselors and ministers are burning out. It is a potential problem, and one that only YOU can solve for yourself.

Here are a few hints that may help prevent burnout, discouragement, or leaving the ministry completely.

SEEK MINISTRY YOURSELF

The most important thing of all in preventing burnout is to seek ministry yourself frequently. The more you give out, the more you need to receive. Seek in-depth inner healing prayer as needed, plus have regular prayer from others often.

I know it will be difficult at times as a counselor to receive ministry for yourself. For one thing, it is hard to find people or groups that can keep confidentiality. Also, if you have a headache (for example) and seek prayer at church or at a healing service, sometimes this inconsequential incident makes the rounds. This simple act of asking for prayer grows and grows, and the rumor may come back two weeks later that you're in the hospital with a brain tumor. Oh, my!

HAVE SUPPORT GROUPS

At the time of the writing of this book I have been praying regularly with two support groups, one consisting of three ladies. Their names (Carolyn, Annette, and Celia — Addie moved away) were given to me one morning specifically by the Lord. When we get together to pray for one another's needs, we know whatever we pray for is a sacred trust and is not to be shared with others.

Another group came about when God told them to come over to love and minister to me when I returned from a month of ministry overseas. I was completely drained and exhausted. God told them to call and say, "We're coming over — I hope you're at home." What a blessing! (Thanks, Lois and Jim, Cheryl and Tom, and Karen.)

YOUR FAMILY SHOULD COME FIRST

If you have children still at home, do not minister every night or every Saturday or Sunday. Those should be family times. Don't break promises to your children in order to minister to someone else.

DON'T LET THE TELEPHONE
RULE YOUR LIFE

Remember, everyone who calls may not be from God, and *you* may not be the one to pray for them.

Unplug the telephone at mealtime. Or get an answering machine. But don't answer the phone during meals or special family times. Don't spend hours on the phone praying or counseling and neglecting your family.

TAKE TIME FOR R & R

If you awaken some morning and *you just don't want to pray with anyone,* don't feel guilty. Don't be alarmed. You're probably just exhausted and you need some time for "R & R" — rest and relaxation. Take a walk; go to the beach; go shopping; take a long nap or do absolutely nothing for a few days. (I still fight guilt feelings anytime I take time off from the office. So, consequently, I don't get as much R & R myself as I desperately need. I pray that God will help me in this area, also.)

I don't know why it is that we in the helping profession (as a whole) will not take time off for rest, relaxation, recharging, rebuilding, and restoration. We can be in the throes of battle fatigue ourselves and yet are hesitant and feel guilty about taking time off for ourselves. God, help us!

LEARN TO SAY NO

Learn to say *no* to whatever God tells you *not* to do. Whether it is a committee meeting at church, *no* to praying with someone for in-depth inner healing, *no* to a speaking engagement, etc. You may say, "Well, I didn't hear God actually say *no.*" If you're "out on your feet," you can rest assured God would want you to take care of His temple — YOU! He gave us common sense to use. (Oh! I just stepped all over my toes, too. Well, praise the Lord anyway!)

LEAVE OF ABSENCE

There may be times you will need to take an extended leave of absence. When my husband, Ed, died, I did not go to the office or counsel for six months. Looking back, I should have taken the extra six months that were advised. We shouldn't be afraid to take extended time off and allow God to minister to us.

TAKE TIME FOR FRIENDS AND FUN

Go out to eat with friends. Just this week friends have helped me celebrate my May 5th birthday. What fun! Sue invited me out to eat at one of my favorite places; I loved hearing all about her daughter's beautiful wedding. Bette Jo and Donna Dee took me to a new restaurant for an out-of-this-world salad. Lois, Cheryl, and Karen took me to the Hyatt for fajitas. When we were together, we had the giggles like four school girls having wonderful, clean fun.

It helps take your mind off newsletter deadlines, or books not finished, your car that's been in the shop 30 days, and all the other numerous problems that are harassing you. Thanks, God, for friends and fun times together.

WATCH FOR SYMPTOMS OF BURNOUT

You certainly don't want to look inward all the time, but it is necessary to watch for the symptoms of burnout in your own life: chronic and severe fatigue, despondency, feeling of hopelessness, depression, inability to get any work done, etc., are just a few of the symptoms of burnout. Don't over-do, over-commit. Take time for yourself; for your own prayer life and meditation, and for your own rest and relaxation. Take time to smell the roses, to have some fun, and enjoy life. Even Jesus went aside to rest and pray.

BIBLE STUDY AND PRAYER

One of the things that brings on burnout, perhaps as much as anything else, is not spending daily, quality time in God's Word and in prayer. Praising God and praying in the Spirit are absolute necessities to keeping your life in balance and in order. The Word says, *"But you, dear friends, must build up your lives ever more strongly upon the foundation of our holy faith, learning to pray in the power and strength of the Holy Spirit"* (Jude 20, TLB).

The Bible says, *"Very early the next morning, long before daylight, Jesus got up and left the house. He went out of town to a lonely place, where he prayed"* (Mark 1:35, St. Jerome).

If Jesus needed quietness and being alone, how much more do we need it, especially in these hectic, and often chaotic, times in which we are living. We must have quality prayer time; we must make it a habit to pray in the Spirit continually all day long. It should be second nature to us. It should be such a part of us that it is like our breathing. It is absolutely imperative to read the Bible every day. That is where we will obtain our spiritual food and strength.

There are tape recorders that reverse the tapes. What a wonderful opportunity to go to sleep at night with Bible tapes playing and having God's Word permeate your entire mind as you sleep. Dr. Judy Fiorentino attributes her miraculous recovery, from a near-fatal airplane crash that left her paralyzed, to the fact that she listened to healing Scriptures twenty-four hours a day.

CHAPTER FOURTEEN

A CALL FROM GOD

"You didn't choose me! I chose you! I appointed you to go and produce lovely fruit always, so that no matter what you ask for from the Father, using my name, he will give it to you" (John 15:16, TLB).

We should KNOW THAT WE KNOW that we have a call from the Lord, and be aware of His leading and anointing before attempting to minister inner healing to someone.

And yet —

My next statement may sound completely opposite from the above statement.

I also believe that EVERYONE — ANYONE may be called to minister at any given time. God is the One in control and the One from Whom the healing power flows. We are only His channel (however rusty). God will not send us "around the world" if we are not willing to go across the street to

140

minister. And we will not always "feel" the anointing. In fact, many times when God's power is the strongest, we feel the weakest.

There are some (fortunately, not many) who have "itchy fingers" to minister. They run in where angels fear to tread. They go "in the flesh," not at the leading and timing of the Holy Spirit.

The Bible says, *"Lay hands suddenly on no man . . ."* (1 Timothy 5:22, KJV). Much harm may be done by not waiting for the voice of the Lord, or by disobeying the voice of the Lord and charging ahead to do your own thing. WE MUST NOT RUN AHEAD OF GOD. . . . WE MUST WAIT ON THE LORD FOR DIRECTIONS AND GUIDANCE.

And yet, on the other hand, neither should we drag our feet. Don't be fearful and filled with inadequacy. When God tells us to "Go," we must go with haste and in confidence. God is calling us to listen and be obedient to Him.

I recall the first time I definitely was aware of hearing the voice of the Lord. It was years ago, when our boys were young teenagers and our daughter a four-year-old. It was five o'clock or so in the afternoon.

Get this picture, if you will.

I was trying to prepare dinner (in Texas we call it supper). I had three things going on the stove at one time: I was boiling potatoes, frying chicken, and cooking green beans. The kids were starving and kept asking, "When is supper ready, Mom?" The phone kept ringing and ringing. Even the cats were hungry and kept meowing at my feet. The dog was whining at the door, saying, "I want something to eat, too." Wow! Total confusion!

Now *that* was the exact moment that God chose to say,

"Betty, I want you to go across the street to see your neighbor, Laverne."

"Okay, Lord," I replied, "I will go right after I get this supper over."

Again, the Lord said, "Betty, I want you to go across the street to see Laverne, *right now.*"

"Yes, Lord, I will, right after I finish feeding the family."

"Betty, GO NOW!" The Lord left no doubt by His tone that *He meant business.*

"Now, Lord?"

"Yes, NOW!"

"Yes, Lord."

I immediately turned off all the burners on the stove, told the kids where I was going, and that I'd be back shortly.

As I was crossing the street, these thoughts were crossing my mind: "What am I doing? What am I going to say to Laverne? Lord, we've only lived in this neighborhood six months. She's going to think I'm crazy when I turn up at her door without a reason."

The doorbell had hardly stopped ringing when Laverne came to the door — *crying.*

"Laverne, what's wrong?" I asked.

"Oh, Betty. Things are just terrible! Weldon, my husband, has a growth on his throat. Our family doctor sent him to a cancer specialist. They both are almost positive it's malignant. He goes into the hospital tomorrow for surgery. We have spent all day going over business papers, insurance policies, and the will."

As she said the word "will" she crumbled.

"Laverne," I heard myself saying, "May I pray that Weldon will be healed?" (Pretty bold for a Baptist gal just baptized in the Holy Spirit, wouldn't you say?)

Her response was, "Oh, yes, please do; please come in."

Her household had the same five o'clock turmoil and confusion that I had just left in my own home. Her troops were "starving," too. So, in order to find a quiet spot, we stepped into the dressing area of their luxurious bathroom. There was no powerful charismatic prayer. Just a heart's cry from a neighbor just baptized in the Spirit who was being obedient to the Lord. "Dear Lord, please heal Weldon."

I prayed for several other things, too. When I finished praying, I asked Laverne what I could do to help with their children, house, pets, etc., while they were at the hospital. (Prayer plus practical helps go hand in hand.)

I walked back across the street, feeling the exhilaration that comes from being an obedient servant. Little did I know what the outcome would be.

The next afternoon, Laverne called from the hospital and excitedly told me, "Betty, it's not cancer; it's not cancer. Your prayer worked!" God healed Weldon!

Then she explained how the family doctor and the cancer surgeon had made their pre-op visit early that morning and explained how serious the surgery would be; that, in all probability, they would have to remove Weldon's vocal cords.

The doctors continued to tell Laverne and Weldon that the surgery would be long. There would be a stay in the recovery room and I.C.U. and not to expect him back in his room for eight hours or so.

The doctors then examined the growth on Weldon's throat. With puzzled expressions, they both muttered, asking one another — "Hmmm, it seems smaller than yesterday, doesn't it?" They then turned and walked toward the door, saying, "Well, we'll see you in surgery," and they left.

Praise the Lord. During the surgery, the doctors found that the growth was only a benign nodule — something that usually only children have. Thank You, Lord Jesus. Weldon was back in his room within two hours. The cancer specialist was a little angry and dismayed at his misdiagnosis. Bless his heart. He didn't misdiagnose. He just was not anticipating the healing power of our Lord.

In looking back at this wonderful miracle, perhaps Weldon would have been healed anyway — but, you know something — look what a blessing *I* would have missed!

I often hear people say, "God doesn't talk to me." Yes, He does; you're not listening! Or,

"God never gives me guidance or tells me to minister to someone." Yes, He does! You probably thought that you were thinking something up. Or, you might think, "Well, that's crazy. I can't go witness to that person. I can't pray that they will be healed."

We must stand on tippy-toes, listening for the still, small voice of the Lord, for His guidance and instructions. We must be obedient and go immediately when He says, "Go." We must realize that *yes, we each have a call on our lives from the Lord.* The Word says, *". . . even so send I you"* (John 20:21, KJV).

145

> **Our credibility as a minister is to wait patiently for God's call, listen to His instructions, and be obedient when they come. And remember, it is our availability — not our ability — that interests the Lord.**

DON'T BE AFRAID

There will be times when the person you are counseling with will have unbelievable problems. Problems that are so severe and complicated. The person even may be demonically oppressed and you're sitting there in front of them — looking confident, calm, and "anointed." But, on the inside you're screaming, "Help, Lord, help! What do I do, Lord?"

When things get rough, do what the picture of the little kitten hanging on to a limb says do, "Hang in there," but you hang in there with Jesus!

When everything seems so complicated and over your head and competence, do what that singing kitchen tea kettle does when the pressure is on and the fire gets hot — it starts singing. We must do the same thing. *But we must sing in the Spirit.*

Seriously, though, and above all, remember:

". . . I can do everything God asks me to with the help of Christ who gives me the strength and power" (Philippians 4:13, TLB).

"If any man lacks wisdom, he should ask God, who gives generously to all . . . and it will be given to him" (James 1:5, NIV).

And don't ever forget that God's Word says, *"You didn't choose me! I chose you! . . ."* (John 15:16, TLB).

KNOW OUR LIMITATIONS

We must recognize and know our limitations.

As a counselor, we must realize that God may not have called us to pray with every person who comes to us for prayer. (When I use the term "pray" I am referring to in-depth inner healing prayer. Of course, we will pray *for* the person, but not always *with.*)

There is a thin line between spiritual knowledge and mental knowledge. We should always rely on and seek first the spiritual knowledge. However, we need to have a basic knowledge of mental illness and be able to recognize when we are dealing with a severely disturbed person who is potentially dangerous to society, his family, or himself.

We need to know our limitations (I didn't say *God's;* I said *ours).* We need to know when to tell the family, "This child needs to be in a safe, loving institution that can minister to him."

147

PRIORITIES

There must be divine order in our lives and ministries and we must have our priorities straight.

If people are calling you constantly on the phone for prayer, knocking at your door daily for prayer, beating a path to your office for inner healing, stopping you after church or at the supermarket and pouring out their heart and asking you for prayer counseling — then — God has indeed placed a call on your life.

You must have a ministry of inner healing, and it's probably time for you to take a good, hard look at your priorities, to see if everything lines up and is in order.

Your priorities should be:

1. God first

2. Family second

3. Ministry third

GOD FIRST

We can become so busy ministering that we don't take time for a quiet time with the Lord in prayer, meditation, and Bible reading. In an earlier book, I wrote that if Satan cannot get us in sin — he will try "busyness." We can also become so wrapped up in our ministry that the ministry is more important than the Deity Who gave it to us.

We must stand guard that no spiritual pride creeps in. We must come before the Lord humbly, repentant, and expectant, and constantly give Him all praise and glory.

We can also be so concerned with our family that we don't take time for God, or to minister to those around us in need.

GOD MUST BE FIRST. It is so vital to have that sweet, precious relationship with our Father. To have that glorious fragrance of His Holy Spirit permeating our lives. We must have a relationship with our Father based on simple trust and obedience. This only comes from prayer, meditation, and fasting.

We must put Him first. *"You shall have no other gods before Me"* (Exodus 20:3, Jerusalem). That includes the possible idols we've made of our family or a ministry.

We must also take time to be fed spiritually ourselves as often as possible. Go to retreats and seminars to be refreshed and rejuvenated with the power of Jesus.

I go to the Charles and Frances Hunter Healing Explosions three or four times a year across the United States, from California to Florida, from Tennessee to Wisconsin.

At these Healing Explosions, held around the world, you are "recharged, energized, and revitalized." There is valuable teaching by Charles and Frances and the Doctors' Panel. I encourage all who are involved in the healing ministry to attend. You'll never be the same. I will add, however, that the Hunter seminars are more on physical healing than emotional healing.

Another place I am spiritually fed is at the national and regional meetings of the Association of Christian Therapists. This organization is made up of doctors, dentists, social workers, psychiatrists, psychologists, Protestant ministers, priests, nuns, nurses, counselors, evangelists, and other professional people who bring the healing Jesus into their profession and who believe in praying for the sick. (At the present, I serve as Secretary to the four-state Region 16 and Fr. Robert DeGrandis is Coordinator for Region 16.)[1]

I especially love and am blessed at the "silent retreats" held at a convent near my home. These quiet times are so special — just to turn my eyes completely on Jesus and listen. Also I recently attended a (Prayer Mountain) Prayer and Fasting Retreat, where I was blessed. These are based on Dr. Cho's ministry from Korea.

As counselors we must continually seek places where we can be fed and ministered to. We need

[1]Fr. DeGrandis and I hold "Healing the Whole Person Seminars." You may call 1-713-558-3703 for information on tapes or write P.O. Box 19827, Houston, Texas 77224 for information.

prayer for inner healing ourselves as often as we can get it. However, nothing takes the place of our own daily quiet time in our prayer room — at home. I praise God for my own special prayer room; the presence of the Holy Spirit is so real there that it is absolutely glorious!

FAMILY SECOND

Unfortunately, there are those occasional, sad cases where the minister's family is completely excluded, neglected, and practically abandoned — all for the cause of a ministry.

When God first thrust me into ministry, I was a substitute teacher at a nearby elementary school. Ed, my husband, was Dean of the Department of Education and Psychology at Houston Baptist University, where he later was elected Academic Vice-President.

At first, we couldn't comprehend the fact that God had thrust me into full-time ministry. The only thing I knew was that my once well-ordered life and house were completely topsy-turvy.

The phone never stopped ringing and someone was always knocking at the door wanting prayer. I found it more and more difficult to keep meals on the table, the shopping done, and clothes and dishes washed.

Finally, one night after I had missed eating with my family several times in a row, I realized something was really wrong. I would be on the kitchen phone praying with someone and watching my family two feet away, eating without me. When I finally got off the phone, they would be finished eating. They had scattered, the food was cold, and I was left with greasy dishes to do — alone.

I did not want to prepare a delicious meal and be ready to sit down to enjoy my family and the meal, only to have a stranger from Kalamazoo call for prayer about something completely inconsequential. Please don't get the wrong impression. I loved the people who called, I loved to pray, I loved to minister, however, I was bewildered and frustrated.

As the ministry expanded, it seemed that Ed and I were praying every night, every Saturday, and Sunday afternoon. We were not spending quality time with our children at all. This situation had to be changed.

Ed and I reorganized our priorities: *Family first.* We cut out almost all nighttime counseling (and I will say it broke our hearts to do so. I battled false guilt for ages). We decided to take the phone off the hook during meals. Later we even had to get an unlisted home number, when I moved into my office ten years ago.

Putting your family first is not always easy.

A Call From God

I recall the time Tammy was in the hospital from a relapse of mononucleosis. I was scheduled to speak at St. Matthew's Episcopal Church. But God started dealing with me about being at the hospital with Tammy that particular night.

"But, Lord, she really isn't that sick — and besides that, all her friends are up there visiting with her at the hospital," I told the Lord.

"Betty," the Lord said, "I want you with Tammy tonight." So I was obedient. Fr. Bill Day was so kind and understanding to encourage me to stay with Tammy at the hospital, and Ed, bless his heart, took the meeting for me.

That night at the hospital I felt a little foolish. Tammy obviously didn't need me. I had been there all day. She wasn't sick, and had gobs of visitors.

Steve[2], my oldest son, and my daughter-in-love, Terry, came in to visit her that night.

Steve, with a wave, said, "Hi, Tammy. How are you?"

"Hi, Steve. Hi, Terry," she said. "It's good to see you!"

[2]Steve is in full-time ministry as founder and director of The Carpenter's Workshop, a state and county approved drug rehabilitation program for heroin addicts. This is a residential program in Houston, Texas, for both men and women. Terry, my daughter-in-love, is involved in medical research at the University of Texas Health Science Center. She is a brilliant, sensitive girl who loves the field of science and looking into microscopes all day hoping to help find a cure for some of today's diseases.

Steve looked at me and said, "Why, hi, Mom! What are you doing here? I thought you had a meeting tonight."

"I did, Son, but your dad took it for me. The Lord told me I should be here with Tammy tonight," I explained.

He paused, grinned, made an okay sign with his fingers, and with a great big smile, slowly said, *"Right on, Mom! Right on!"*

I'll never know or understand the significance of this episode — but at least I was obedient to the Lord. When He said, "Put your child first" — I did!

I recall another incident. I had spoken for two days in Ohio. The closing session was a banquet where I was to speak. All day long I had felt such an urgency in my spirit. There was such an unsettled feeling. I knew something was wrong with the family.

I called the University where Ed was Vice-President to see if everything was okay at home. Ed's Executive Secretary, Mrs. Blacklock, said, "Betty, Ed went home from work. He is very sick." I started trying to reach Ed at home and couldn't (he had disconnected the phone because he felt so bad and desperately needed to get some sleep). I've never agonized over a decision more — but I felt, "I absolutely MUST get home. I must." I explained to Pastor Don, my church host. Bless his heart, he understood that I felt I had to leave for home immediately, that something was seriously wrong.

When I arrived home, I found Ed the sickest I had seen him in 25 years of marriage. My place was with him as a loving and caring wife. Thank you, pastor, for allowing me to keep my priorities straight.

Let me hasten to say that, as ministers, we are to be absolutely dependable — not canceling meetings or appointments right and left. However, when our family needs us — they need US! It may not be just when they are sick either.

For example: Tammy[3] was ten years old, when for about two weeks it seemed as if I did nothing but pray for someone all day and into the night. It was in the early days of ministry, when our office was the living room. It seemed that I was always in there, praying for someone.

I could tell that Tammy was feeling neglected and unloved. My heart ached for her and for me, too.

"Honey, how would you like to go shopping this afternoon?" I asked.

She smiled, her spirits lifted. "Oh! Mom, I'd love to!" she exclaimed.

[3]Tammy is a beautiful, Spirit-filled young woman of 23. She is finishing her Masters in Management and is secretary to the Dean of Business at Houston Baptist University. She has a very gentle, compassionate spirit. She belongs to an organization that cares for wounded and homeless animals. (St. Francis would be pleased. You could never guess how many animals we have had at one given time.)

She barely had the words out of her mouth when the phone rang. A hysterical stranger was on the other end.

The lady said, "I absolutely MUST see you RIGHT NOW! It positively cannot wait!"

"I'm sorry but I have other commitments," I said gently.

"No," she said, "I have to see you right now. I can't wait."

"Well, I'm sorry," I patiently explained. "I've a commitment with my daughter. I can see you in the morning." After a few more sentences and a prayer, I hung up.

Imagine my astonishment when Tammy said, "Mother, how could you turn that lady down? She needed you this afternoon. We can go shopping later."

"Tammy, I want to spend time with you" (not voicing it, but feeling that we desperately needed to be together). "You need me today just as much as that lady does."

"Mom, call her back," my ten-year-old said with such maturity, "and pray for her this afternoon. We can go shopping tonight." And that's what we did. Tammy just needed to know that she was the most important thing in my life.

The only other time that I've had to miss a meeting because of my family concerned my middle son, Paul.[4] He is a lawyer with a prestigious firm in Houston, and is married to my daughter-in-love, Barbara.

While Paul was in law school, one particular week before finals, there was a crazy, incredible, episode fraught with potential disaster.

Paul called to explain his situation. "Son, would you like for me to come?" I asked. "Mom, could you?" he responded.

I had been scheduled to hold an inner healing seminar at a particular church for six months. But as I prayed, the Lord said, "You are to go to be with your son." I called the pastor of the church where I was to speak and shared some of the situation.

"Betty," he said, "I agree. You need to be with your son." Then he added, "I've always heard preachers say, 'Put your family before a church meeting,' but you're the first one I know who actually has done so. Betty, you have my love, prayers, and blessings."

I hung up the phone with a thankful heart.

---

[4]At the time of this writing, Paul leads the worship music at church at the 8:00 a.m. service. He often plays the French Horn in the orchestra at 9:00 a.m. Then at 10:45 a.m. he team-teaches a Sunday school class. Barbara sings in the choir, or plays the handbells or flute in the orchestra. They are back at church at 5:00 p.m. Sunday. I've felt a need to admonish them to stay in balance, even in church. (What a thing for a mom to do.)

Our family must never feel that the whole world is more important than they are, that everyone else's problems and concerns come before our family. This includes our parents, as well. They all need to know that God is first, they are second, and that the ministry is third.

MINISTRY THIRD

It is not easy to stay in balance. In fact, it is extremely difficult to juggle all the demands on your time. But we must strive to stay in balance.

There will be times when you will make the wrong choice; times when you should have chosen the family over the ministry.

If you don't have a full-time staff or office, you will find that inevitably a person in need will call at night when your family also needs you. There will be times you feel pulled in a million different directions.

In times like these, you need the wisdom of Solomon and the patience of Job to know which comes first. Always seek the Lord, but remember He gave those children to you as your main ministry and priority.

Unfortunately, I do need to add just a note. As a counselor, you will find that there will be an occasional caller who is very selfish and self-centered!

Their problems may not be an emergency, or even serious at all. They may be a lonely, angry, confused person seeking attention, and looking for someone to whom they can vent their negative feelings. To them, their problem is the most important thing in the world. Especially in cases like this, you have to have levels of priority concerning with whom the Lord would have you pray.

I recall an incident which occurred years ago in the first years of the ministry. A lady in tears, called early one morning. She was very agitated and upset and kept saying, "I don't know what to do. I don't know what to do. . . ."

"About what?" I inquired.

"Oh!" she said, "neither my maid nor my gardener can come today to help me. They come every day but can't come today. I don't know what I'll do!"

I just held the phone, sighed, and thought, "I can't believe this." I looked over at my sink with dishes piled high, and no time to do them because I had been praying for people "around the clock." A gardener! Oh, my — I'd love to have just enough time to plant a few petunias in my own yard.

I prayed for the stranger. But I'll be honest — I'm not certain my attitude was quite right. Then I said to her, "Would you pray for me? I'm up to my ears in household chores and duties left undone while praying for others. Please pray that God will help *me* get everything done."

You, as the counselor, must establish the levels of priority within the ministry. You do so with firmness but compassion, always exercising your Christian wisdom. Some of your priorities may become stationary; others are constantly shifting.

As your ministry grows, you will have less and less time to do all the things you need to do or want to do — write books, return phone calls, prayer counseling, answer letters, speak at meetings, hold seminars, attend meetings to be fed spiritually yourself, visit family and friends — or wonder of wonders — take a vacation.

There may even come a time in your ministry that you're looking for just an extra fifteen minutes — say, to eat, go to the cleaners, or Glory — take a walk around the block!

God knows the attitude of our heart. He loves a contrite heart. Some duties that we think are so important may not be important to God at all.

Some things that we may consider trivial may be the key to His heart. For example: Stopping during your morning walk to talk and listen to an elderly neighbor who is so lonely and yearns for someone with whom to chat.

Nothing, absolutely nothing can be as important as taking the time to call your parents (and in-laws) to check to see how they are, to tell them about your activities, and to tell them that you love them.

Besides God, there is no greater priority than your family and Christian friends. Take time to go out to eat, share fun and laughter together. Keep family commitments.

Praise God for the call that God places on each of our lives. But a call from God — out of balance and misshapen, and a call from God with our priorities all warped and bent, is a sad state of affairs.

DOES GOD CALL COLLECT?

Is there a price to pay when you receive a CALL FROM THE LORD? Yés, there *IS* a price when you say "yes" to being in His full-time service.

Much, much time must be spent in prayer, meditation (listening), and in the Bible. We must have a servant's heart and a willingness to say, *"Yes, Lord"* — *whatever the cost.*

There must be a willingness to be an obedient handmaiden or servant of the Lord. We must always be willing to do the Lord's will, and not ours. We must die to self. We have to let the Holy Spirit direct our lives completely.

There is a cost; there is a price to pay when you are called. For one thing, it places you on the front line of spiritual warfare. It is not always easy. You may receive much harassment from the enemy. There may be many trials and tribulations.

But I say —

— "Praise the Lord" for His call.

— "Glory to God" for being His instrument.

— "Hallelujah" for being able to walk in this glorious, magnificent, and miraculous walk.

Is there a cost when God calls you? Yes! But He reimburses the cost a million times over.

Thank You, Lord, for Your call.

Make This Your Own Personal Prayer

Oh, Lord Jesus, how I love You and thank You for the call that You have placed on my life. Lord, thank You for Your anointing, Your revelation knowledge and the gifts that You have made available.

Dear God, make me worthy of this call. Give me wisdom and guidance. May I have the mind of Christ. Make me sensitive to Your voice. Give me such a desire to always be instantly obedient to do Your will. Lord, give me common sense and help me to keep my priorities straight. And Lord, most of all, may I always keep my eyes on You. Help me to always put You first in my life.

May I always place my precious family before duty, work, obligations, or even the ministry.

May the ministry You have called me to always bring honor and glory to You. May my spirit always be gentle and humble. Dear Lord, let there always be divine order in every area of my life.

I love You, Lord, and I lift my voice to You to say I give You all praise and glory for the wondrous things that You do. Thank You for Your Call. In Jesus' name. A m e n .

This is what Yahweh asks of you . . .
to act justly
to love tenderly
to walk humbly —
with your God.

                                    Micah 6:8

As you pray for people, many will be healed *spiritually* (the greatest and most important healing of all). Many will be healed *emotionally,* and you will rejoice and praise God for the changed lives.

Others will be healed *physically.* How wonderful to see cancer, M.S., and arthritis healed by Jesus. How glorious to see a cancerous growth the size of a grapefruit on a lady's throat shrink away. (And in the process of seeing Jesus heal his wife, her agnostic doctor husband accepted Christ.) How wonderful to see God heal a deaf mute in Costa Rica and hear her say for the first time, "I love You, Jesus" in perfect English, a language that she did not know, and not in her native Spanish.

How exciting to witness God's healing of a tumor in a friend's ear. Tapscott Ministries rents our office from Gail and her husband, Ed. She was diagnosed as having a tumor growing deep within her ear. It caused severe dizziness. Many people were praying. We prayed for her several times and also anointed her with oil. Four days after it was first diagnosed, she was sent to a specialist. His report was that *no* tumor showed up on the x-ray, as it had earlier. He could find no tumor! There was jubilation in the office when Gail and Ed came in to tell us. Praise the Lord for His mighty healing power.

But, not everyone is healed.

There may come a time when the Lord will say (as He did to me one day), "I've healed Eva spiritually; I've healed her emotionally; but I'm calling her home to be with Me to heal her physically."

The following is Eva's story.

CHAPTER FIFTEEN

THE STORY OF EVA

*Our Role as a Counselor May Be At Times to
"Walk Home With the Counselee So They
Won't Be Afraid."*

Charlotte, my beauty operator, was the one who asked me to pray for her friend, Eva.

I still remember the day Charlotte said, "Betty, Eva has cancer and has been told by her doctor that she only has a few days to live. Can she come to your office for prayer?"

Charlotte was from Hungary. She escaped with her uncle from there during the revolution. Eva was also a Hungarian refugee.

Eva arrived at my office in two or three days. She had read my book, *Inner Healing Through Healing of Memories,* that Charlotte had passed on to her to read.

When Eva entered the office, I noticed how terribly thin she was. Her skin had a yellowish color. She

165

was very weak and in pain.

After she was seated in my office, we had a word of prayer to ask the Lord to direct and bless our time together.

Then I asked her the question I ask all counselees, "Do you know Jesus as your personal Saviour?"

"Well," she answered, "my name is on the church roll at my church."

"No, that's not what I mean. If Jesus were to come right now, do you know that you know that you would go to be with Him?"

She paused a moment, and then honestly answered, "No, I don't have that assurance."

So, the first order of business was to lead her in the sinner's prayer, and have her ask forgiveness of all her sins and to ask Jesus Christ into her heart as Saviour. Praise the Lord!

As she did this, there was a precious release of the Spirit on her that was evident in the glow in her eyes.

Then I said, "Eva, tell me about yourself. Give me a 'thumbnail' sketch of your life."

She had been in Hungary during the uprising. Her young husband had been killed in this revolution. Her baby was born in an air raid shelter. For what reason I was never sure of, she left her son with her parents and escaped to America.

Shortly after arriving in the United States, she met and married a man. They had so much in common: love for the arts, opera, ballet, etc.

But it was not too long after their marriage that she developed cancer. For seventeen years she fought this battle, a battle of surgery, chemotherapy, radiation, x-rays, pain, hospital stays, and medical bills.

Her husband, somewhere in those seventeen years, became disenchanted and disgusted with Eva's long battle of cancer. He left Eva for her best friend (who was also married, with four children) and they went to live in another country.

My heart broke for Eva as she finished her story with a shrug of her shoulders and a movement of her hand that displayed complete futility and hopelessness.

I explained to Eva how I would pray for the healing of her wounded spirit: I would pray asking the Lord to set her free from depression, grief, loneliness, jealousy, fear, unforgiveness, and any other unholy spirits that had come against her. I told her that it was not bringing up garbage, but throwing away the garbage that was there.

I shared how I would ask Jesus to cleanse and heal all her emotional wounds — to take a spiritual eraser and wipe away the hurt of the painful memories. I explained to her the importance of forgiveness, that it was the key to wholeness. I also told her that forgiveness was an act of the will, and not a feeling. I knew that it would be very difficult to forgive her husband and her best friend.

Then I prayed the inner healing prayer for her. There was much crying and release in her spirit as she introduced Jesus Christ into every one of those hurts. We prayed from before she was born to the present time.

We asked Jesus to fill all the voids in her life, to restore what the locusts had eaten (see Joel 2:25, TLB).

"Oh," she said, "I'm feeling so much lighter!"

"We're not through praying yet, Eva. God is not through touching you."

"Eva, would you like to receive the baptism in the Holy Spirit?" I asked.

"Oh! Yes," she responded, "I want everything God has for me."

She soon was praying in a beautiful prayer language.

I called my two secretaries into the room. I said, "Join me as I anoint Eva with oil and ask the Lord to touch her so she will 'rest in the Spirit.' "

As Eva was resting in the Spirit, Lois, Elizabeth, and I watched the most incredible phenomenon.

The Story of Eva

We noticed "something" begin to move in her abdomen, move up into the chest area, and we watched as "something" left Eva's body.

Elizabeth said, "I felt a cold wind just go by me."

Eva exclaimed, "I'm healed! I'm healed! Oh, I feel just great! All the pain is gone. Oh, praise God! I feel wonderful."

We were all rejoicing with her. The power of the Lord was so strong that we could barely stand up in the room. We were laughing, crying, and praising God, all at the same time.

Before Eva left, I encouraged her to start attending New Testament Fellowship church where Lois and her husband, Jim, were pastors.

"Eva, you must put on the whole armor of God. Pray in the Spirit without ceasing, continuously forgive your husband and your best friend, and above all, keep constantly praising God."

We all assured her that if she needed us, night or day, all she had to do was call.

She looked like a new and different person as she walked out the door of my office.

Then — I heard the voice of the Lord.

"Betty, I've healed her spiritually and emotionally, but I'm taking her home to be with Me."

I shared with my two secretaries what I heard the Lord say. They responded with, "No — oh, no, that couldn't be. We've never felt the power of the Lord more. We actually saw 'something' leave her body. We saw how she was free of pain and was filled with energy. Oh, no! She must be healed."

I prayed that they were right, and that I had heard wrong.

Eva started attending their small charismatic church and became a loyal member. She blessed others with her testimony, and was blessed herself by all the precious warmth and love showered upon her by the members in New Testament Fellowship.

Almost three months passed when Eva started having pain again. She was readmitted to the hospital.

The prognosis — death in a matter of days. She was in incredible pain. People continued to pray, visit her in the hospital, take her flowers, fruit, and send cards.

Then something marvelous happened to her one night. Eva had a wonderful experience with the Lord.

It was two o'clock in the morning. There she was, in the hospital, receiving pain medication through the I.V.'s in both arms — all alone — her husband and best friend together in another country. She was feeling utter rejection and loneliness.

"But Betty," Eva told me later, "I did what you told me to do. I started praying in the Spirit. I prayed and prayed and prayed in the Spirit. Soon, a beautiful, supernatural glow came into my room. I felt the presence of the Lord in a powerful, glorious way. Oh," she continued, "I felt such peace. *And I've never felt more loved than at that moment.*"

A few days later, Eva died. Our hearts were broken: "God, I don't understand. Why, Lord? Why did she die? What was this all about, Lord? We saw the spirit of cancer leave her. We saw her walk in health and victory for two months. What happened, God?"

Very gently, God answered,

"Betty, do you remember when you were a kid, and you were down the street, playing with your playmates? Do you remember the times when it became dark and your mother would come to the door and call out, 'Come on home, Betty — supper's ready'? Do you remember, Betty," God continued, *"how your little playmates would say, 'We'll walk home with you so you won't be afraid'?"*

"Yes, Lord, I remember."

"Well, my child, I called you into Eva's life and called those other Christians from New Testament church into Eva's life to love her, to care for her, to be a friend to her and: TO WALK HOME WITH HER SO SHE WOULDN'T BE AFRAID."

This is what God is calling each of us to do.

Most of the people we pray with for salvation will come to know Jesus. Many of the people you pray with for emotional healing will be healed by the Lord. Many of the people you pray with for physical healing will receive either total or partial healing. But — there will be some who will not be healed physically. God is calling them home where they will receive that total and perfect eternal healing.

Our job, our Divine Commission in cases like this is to:

> *"walk*
>
> > *home*
> >
> > > *with*
> > >
> > > > *them*
> > > >
> > > > > *so*
> > > > >
> > > > > > *they*
> > > > > >
> > > > > > > *won't*
> > > > > > >
> > > > > > > > *be*
> > > > > > > >
> > > > > > > > > *afraid."*

APPENDIX I

PSYCHOLOGY/CHURCH COUNSELING?

Question: *Does the work of a professional counseling psychologist conflict with his being an evangelical Christian?*

There is no need for Christians to fear the developing science and art of psychology — which by definition is simply "the study of behavior." On the contrary, psychology should be viewed as any other human endeavor — an opportunity and responsibility to honor and glorify The Creator, Jesus Christ Himself. Remember, *". . . all things were created by him and for him"* (Colossians 1:16).

No greater psychologist ever practiced than Jesus Christ Himself. He routinely utilized effective interpersonal principles and techniques long before mankind "discovered" them through government-sponsored research projects. For example, Jesus demonstrated the need for a counselor to adapt and use different methods when dealing with individual situations: Jesus listened and talked to many;

173

He laughed with some and He cried with some; He touched some; He consoled many; He was typically forgiving and supportive, but was sometimes confrontational and demanding. As a counselor, Jesus was always personal and adaptable.

The Master Psychologist Jesus Christ also taught the need for individuals to confess their sins; He recognized the therapeutic value of both seeking and providing forgiveness. These and similar biblically based mental health principles frequently are announced "breakthroughs" in academic dissertations, in "how to" books on daily living, and on TV talk shows.

While some psychological knowledge is helpful in Christian living, there are some matters related to psychology which are oppositional to Christ, do not honor Him, and should be avoided. For example, evangelical Christians must shun psychology which is linked with humanism, a Christ-rejecting ideology which has the characteristics of a false religion. Individual spiritual growth requires that we each assume responsibility for embracing the truth while rejecting false knowledge. God has endowed us with wonderfully unique resources like the mind and the will; the authority and responsibility for maximizing these precious resources rests squarely with each individual.

Dr. Charles R. Poor, Psychologist
Counseling Ministry Director
First Baptist Church
Houston, Texas

BASIC GUIDELINES FOR INNER HEALING

1. Keep all inner healing ministry grounded in the Bible and based on Jesus Christ. As a minister of inner healing, spend much time in prayer and in reading the Bible. Always strive to be a mature, stable Christian, one who brings honor to Jesus.

2. Keep your eyes on Jesus and not on Satan. Remember Christians cannot be possessed, only oppressed. Don't look for a demon behind every door or a spirit behind every sneeze.

3. Keep your healing of memories prayer simple and not saturated with symbolism.

4. Inner healing is a process, not a one-time experience.

5. Never encourage a person to discontinue prescribed medication. We are not doctors — but prayer counselors. Have all physical and emotional healings verified.

6. Keep telling the counselee, or others with whom you are sharing, that inner healing is "Jesus Christ binding up wounds and healing broken hearts" (Psalm 143:3, TLB).

7. Inner healing must never hint of anything psychic, New Age, Humanistic, or the Eastern religions.

8. Forgiveness is the key to inner healing. There must always be true repentance.

9. Above all — *keep expecting miracles.* If you're in an air conditioned room, you get cool. If you're in a heated room, you get warm. So any time there is prayer — expect the person to be touched by Jesus in some manner — spirit, soul, or body.

10. Remember to minister in:
    Balance . . . Love . . . Truth.

SCRIPTURES ON INNER HEALING

All quotations are from the Living Bible unless noted otherwise.

Isaiah 53:5: *". . . He was wounded and bruised for our sins. He was chastised that we might have peace; he was lashed — and we were healed!"*

Romans 12:2, KJV: *"And be not conformed to this world: but be ye transformed by the renewing of your mind."*

John 14:27: *"I am leaving you with a gift — peace of mind and heart! And the peace I give isn't fragile like the peace the world gives. So don't be troubled or afraid."*

Luke 10:27: *". . . you must love the Lord your God with all your heart, and with all your soul, and with all your strength, and with all your mind. . . ."*

Colossians 1:13-14: *"For he has rescued us out of the darkness and gloom of Satan's kingdom and brought us into the kingdom of his dear Son, who* bought our freedom with his blood and forgave us all our sins.''

2 Corinthians 3:17, KJV: *''Now the Lord is that Spirit: and where the Spirit of the Lord is, there is liberty.''*

Matthew 18:18: *''. . . whatever you bind on earth is bound in heaven, and whatever you free on earth will be freed in heaven.''*

Hebrews 13:8: *''Jesus Christ is the same yesterday, today, and forever.''*

Philippians 3:13: *''Forgetting the past and looking forward to what lies ahead.''*

Hebrews 4:12: *''For whatever God says to us is full of living power; it is sharper than the sharpest dagger, cutting swift and deep into our innermost thoughts and desires with all their parts, exposing us for what we really are.''*

Hebrews 4:13: *''He knows about everyone, everywhere. Everything about us is bare and wide open to the all-seeing eyes of our living God; nothing can be hidden from him to whom we must explain all that we have done.''*

Exodus 20:5, KJV: *''. . . I the Lord thy God am a jealous God, visiting the iniquity of the fathers upon the children unto the third and fourth generation of them that hate me.''*

John 14:12, KJV: *''Verily, verily, I say unto you, He that believeth on me, the works that I do shall he do also; and greater works than these shall he do; because I go unto my Father.''*

Ephesians 3:16: *''. . . out of his glorious, unlimited resources he will give you the mighty inner strengthening of his Holy Spirit.''*

1 Peter 1:22: *"Now you can have real love for everyone because your souls have been cleansed from selfishness and hatred when you trusted Christ to save you. . . .''*

Matthew 12:35-36, Phillips: *''. . . A good man gives out good — from the goodness stored in his heart; a bad man gives out evil — from his store of evil.''*

James 4:7: *"So give yourselves humbly to God. Resist the devil and he will flee from you.''*

Hebrews 12:15: *''. . . Watch out that no bitterness takes root among you, for as it springs up it causes deep trouble, hurting many in their spiritual lives.''*

Luke 10:19: *''. . . I have given you authority over all the power of the Enemy, and to walk among serpents and scorpions and to crush them. Nothing shall injure you!''*

Malachi 4:6: *"His preaching will bring fathers and children together again, to be of one mind and heart. . . .''*

Psalm 51:10: *"Create in me a new, clean heart, O God, filled with clean thoughts and right desires.''*

Scriptures on Inner Healing

Psalm 147:3: *"He heals the brokenhearted, binding up their wounds."*

Galatians 5:22-23: *"But when the Holy Spirit controls our lives he will produce this kind of fruit in us: love, joy, peace, patience, kindness, goodness, faithfulness, gentleness and self-control. . . ."*

Ephesians 2:14: *"For Christ himself is our way of peace. . . ."*

Isaiah 26:3: *"He will keep in perfect peace all those who trust in him, whose thoughts turn often to the Lord!"*

Luke 4:18-19: *"The Spirit of the Lord is upon me . . . he has sent me to heal the brokenhearted and to announce that captives shall be released and the blind shall see, that the downtrodden shall be freed from their oppressors, and that God is ready to give blessings to all who come to him."*

1 Thessalonians 5:23: *"May the God of peace himself make you entirely pure and devoted to God; and may your spirit and soul and body be kept strong and blameless until that day when our Lord Jesus Christ comes back again."*

1 Peter 5:8: *"Be careful — watch out for attacks from Satan, your great enemy. He prowls around like a hungry, roaring lion, looking for some victim to tear apart."*

Psalm 116:16-17: *"O Lord, you have freed me from my bonds and I will serve you forever. I will worship you and offer you a sacrifice of thanksgiving."*

Isaiah 9:4: *"For God will break the chains that bind his people and the whip that scourges them. . . ."*

Jeremiah 6:14: *"You can't heal a wound by saying it's not there! . . ."*

Jeremiah 40:4: *"Now I am going to take off your chains and let you go. . . ."*

Jeremiah 30:17: *"I will give you back your health again and heal your wounds. . . ."*

Ephesians 6:12: *"For we are not fighting against people made of flesh and blood, but against persons without bodies — the evil rulers of the unseen world, those mighty satanic beings and great evil princes of darkness who rule this world; and against huge numbers of wicked spirits in the spirit world."*

John 8:36: *"So if the Son sets you free, you will indeed be free. . . ."*

Psalm 139:13-16: *"You made all the delicate, inner parts of my body, and knit them together in my mother's womb. Thank you for making me so wonderfully complex! It is amazing to think about. Your workmanship is marvelous — and how well I know it. You were there while I was being formed in utter seclusion! You saw me before I was born and scheduled each day of my life before I began to breathe. Every day was recorded in your Book!"*

Isaiah 43:4: *". . . you are precious to me and honored, and I love you."*

Proverbs 26:22, Amp.: *"The words of a whisperer or a slanderer are as dainty morsels or words of sport to some but to others are as deadly wounds, and they go down into the innermost parts of the body."*

Romans 8:1: *"So there is now no condemnation awaiting those who belong to Christ Jesus."*

Proverbs 14:30, RSV: *"A tranquil mind gives life to the flesh."*

Isaiah 42:3: *"He will not break the bruised reed, nor quench the dimly burning flame. He will encourage the fainthearted, those tempted to despair. . . ."*

Isaiah 49:15, St. Jerome: *"Can a woman forget her own baby and not love the child she bore? Even if a mother should forget her child, I will never forget you. . . ."*

3 John 1:2: *"Dear friend, I am praying that all is well with you and that your body is as healthy as I know your soul is."*

APPENDIX IV

RECOMMENDED READING

Bennett, Rita. *How to Pray for Inner Healing for Yourself and Others.* Old Tappan, New Jersey: Fleming H. Revell Company, 1984.

_____ . *Making Peace With Your Inner Child.* Old Tappan, New Jersey: Fleming H. Revell Company, 1987.

Bennett, Dennis and Rita. *Trinity of Man.* Plainfield, New Jersey: Logos International, 1979.

DeGrandis, Rev. Robert. *The Gift of Prophecy.* 1911 Law St., New Orleans, Louisiana 70119, 1984.

_____ . *Forgiveness and Inner Healing*[1]. 1911 Law St., New Orleans, Louisiana 70119, 1980.

_____ . *Healing of Self-Image*[2]. 1911 Law St., New Orleans, Louisiana 70119, 1986.

[1]Coauthored with Betty Tapscott.
[2]*Ibid.*

182

Recommended Reading

Dobson, Theodore E. *How to Pray for Spiritual Growth.* New York/Ramsey: Paulist Press, 1982.

Feider, Rev. Paul A. *The Journey to Inner Peace.* Notre Dame, Indiana 46556: Ave Maria Press, 1984.

Linn, Dennis; Linn, Matthew; and Fabricant, Sheila. *Praying With Another for Healing.* New York/Ramsey: Paulist Press, 1984.

McDonald, Dr. Robert L. *Memory Healing.* Atlanta, Georgia: RLM Ministries, Inc., 1981.

Messenger, M.D., David L. *Dr. Messenger's Guide to Better Health.* Old Tappan, New Jersey: Fleming H. Revell Company, 1981.

Payne, Leane. *The Healing of the Homosexual.* Westchester, Illinois: Crossway Books, 1985.

Seamands, David A. *Healing for Damaged Emotions.* Wheaton, Illinois: Victor Books, 1981.

_____ . *Putting Away Childish Things.* Wheaton, Illinois: Victor Books, 1982.

_____ . *Healing of Memories.* Wheaton, Illinois: Victor Books, 1985.

Shlemon, Barbara Leahy. *Healing the Hidden Self.* Notre Dame, Indiana: Ave Maria Press, 1982.

Tapscott, Betty. *Inner Healing Through Healing of Memories.* Houston, Texas: Tapscott Ministries, 1975.

———. *Set Free Through Inner Healing.* Kingwood, Texas: Hunter Books, 1978.

———. *The Fruit of the Spirit.* Kingwood, Texas: Hunter Books, 1978.

———. *Out of the Valley.* Nashville, Tennessee: Thomas Nelson Publishers, 1980.

———. *Forgiveness and Inner Healing*[3]. Houston, Texas: Tapscott Ministries, 1980.

———. *Healing of Self-Image*[4]. Houston, Texas: Tapscott Ministries, 1986.

Verny, M.D., Thomas; with Kelly, John. *The Secret Life of the Unborn Child.* New York, New York: Dell Publishing Co., Inc., 1982.

Wheeler, Fr. Jim. *School for Spiritual Growth and Inner Healing.* St. Joseph Prayer Center, 4900 Sequoia, NW, Albuquerque, New Mexico 87140.

[3]Coauthored with Rev. Robert DeGrandis.
[4]*Ibid.*

ABOUT THE AUTHOR

Betty Stevens Tapscott (an ordained minister) is an internationally known author and speaker. Her books are published in German, Portuguese and Spanish. She has ministered in Canada, England, Costa Rica, Belize, Mexico, Panama, and Germany. She is a member of the Association of Christian Therapists.

Mrs. Tapscott ministers powerfully with the anointing of Jesus Christ in the area of Healing the Whole Person: Spirit, Soul and Body. The ministry is well balanced and soundly based on the Biblical principles laid down by Jesus Christ. The main emphasis of the ministry is the miracle of healing that comes through forgiveness, reconciliation and restoration.

Mrs. Tapscott has three grown children, plus two "daughters-in-love." She is a widow. Dr. Ed Tapscott, Academic Vice President of Houston Baptist University, died September, 1983.

Before being called by God into full-time ministry over a decade ago, she was a teacher and had a nationally syndicated children's television program. She and her husband were of Southern Baptist background and were filled with the Spirit April 25, 1972. She has B.A. and M.Ed. degrees.

Mrs. Tapscott is ecumenical, speaking through the years in many different Christ-centered churches. She has been the featured speaker at many Aglow State Conventions. She is often on TV and radio, and has written for magazines.

Her main goal is to always lift up Jesus Christ and give Him praise and glory for the miracles He performs.

She ministers in balance, truth, power, yet gentleness. She radiates the love and joy of Jesus Christ.

To order books and tapes, write to:
BETTY TAPSCOTT
P.O. Box 19827, Houston, Texas 77224